Hidden in Plain Sight

Identifying Our Little Foxes

By Alicia Beattie

and

HelenAnn Williams Baillie

Hidden in Plain Sight: Identifying Our Little Foxes

© 2022 by Alicia Beattie and HelenAnn Williams Baillie.

Photo credit for HelenAnn's author picture: Mary Gorman.

ISBNs: 979-8-9872676-0-8 (Paperback)

979-8-9872676-1-5 (Ebook)

Printed in the United States of America.

Dedication

from Alicia

I dedicate this book to my miracle twins: William Isaac and Alexander. May you always walk in your full calling and anointing and live in victory.

from HelenAnn

To Maggie, Richie, Alice, and Sadie Ann: Never forget how powerful your voice is—and never forget the One who died to give you that authority.

Acknowledgments

From Alicia:

Writing a book is both a labor of love and a rewarding task. I never imagined what I would go through to birth this book. It came forth from some of the most intense battles I have ever faced. The Enemy threw everything he could at me. I cannot tell a lie: I dealt with everything from marital problems to kids with RSV and everything in between. That being said, I have some very special thanks I need to share.

I would like to give a very special thank you to my dear friend and sister in Christ, Elsie Williamson. You were there for me in the worst times and trials of my life, lifting me up and acting as a true friend. I am not sure there would even be a book if it wasn't for you. When I wanted to give up, you told me to keep going. We prayed together, fellowshipped together. You are the definition of a true Christian, and I couldn't be happier to call you, my friend. I love you and hope you know you are a very real piece of this book. Never quit being you.

I would also like to thank my husband. He always tells me there is nothing, in Christ, that I cannot do, and he spent countless hours watching our twins so I could type, write, edit, and format. He never complained or questioned it, and never asked for thanks. It was extra time I desperately needed.

I'd like to thank my church, New Life House of Worship. You took me in and gave me a church to call home. You showed me how to have freedom in the Spirit, and what true Christian love looks like. I am so glad my children will have the opportunity to learn from you. Thank you for teaching us how to always make room and give time for the Spirit to have his way. I know I have grown from sitting under you. I love you, Pastor Johnny Smith, and Pastor Jimmy Townsley and all our leadership. We are a true family.

Thank you, HelenAnn, for taking this journey with me, and to my Armed and Anointed team, for all you do. To Lisa Hicks for always being there to guide me and direct me. You have been my spiritual advisor whenever I needed you. To Marzella for being a spiritual guide as well You may not even realize it, but my spiritual gifting grew through our prayer lines. And to my Frontlines ladies: I love every one of you. I am here and able to do what I do thanks to each and every one of you in my life.

Last but not least, to my sister, Irene McMillan, who without a second thought when technology failed, sent her tablet so I could get this done and keep it on schedule. You are the best sister and aunt, and you have the best heart, always thinking of others before yourself. I couldn't imagine life without you. God made you special just for me. He knew I was going to need you as my little sister to do life.

From HelenAnn:

This project is an answered prayer of mine, and I am beyond thankful for this door the Lord has opened for me. I want to thank Alicia for being obedient and asking me to help, without even knowing that this was something I dreamed of doing. I will forever be thankful for your obedience.

I want to thank my parents, Richie and MargaretAnn, who have spoken this into my life ever since I was eighteen years old when I first told them I wanted to write books. They always spoke life into this desire, and I was never ashamed to tell people that I planned to be writing books one day. Thank you for lighting the fire for this passion and rekindling it when I thought it would burn out. Thank you for always encouraging me to be who God created me to be. Otherwise, I would never have picked up a pen.

I want to thank my big brother, Richard, for sowing into my writing dreams by buying my laptop for the sole purpose of writing books and telling me this: "A slow laptop is not a good enough excuse to give up on your dreams. Giving up is never an option. You have to put in the work." Your encouragement made a difference.

To my other brothers, George and Robert, and my sister-in-law, Sadie, I am beyond blessed to be part of a family that fully supports me in anything I set out to do—no matter how farfetched it may seem. You all spoke life and always encouraged me to not give up, even when the road seemed uncertain, and I didn't know if this was possible. Look where we are now! I wouldn't be writing this now if it hadn't had been for my family cheering me on for the past ten years. And for that I will be forever thankful.

Thank you to my husband, Willie, for helping me stay focused on this project while we navigated our new season of marriage together. He helped me keep my eyes first on the kingdom and reminded me that when your eyes are on Christ, everything else will fall into place. Thank you for encouraging me when I felt like I was unqualified to do what I was called to do and keeping me humble when my pride started to show. Thanks for making me go to bed and take breaks so I didn't overwork myself, and for calling me out on my procrastination. I love you so much and could not have finished this project without you.

Lastly, thank you, Marzella and Daisy, for building me up in the Lord. You don't realize how much confirmation you provided that helped strengthen my faith to move forward. Thank you to all the Frontline women for always encouraging me and pouring into me. A big thank you to all my friends, you know who you are, who have supported me, checked in on our progress, and basically pumped me up. I love you all so much. I am blessed and thankful that God placed you all in my life. I would not be here now if it were not for your support.

Catch the foxes for us—
the little foxes that ruin the vineyards—
for our vineyards are in bloom.

—Song of Solomon 2:15

Contents

The Angel of Light
by HelenAnn

Out in the open for everyone to see,
No one is scared, especially not me.

What a beautiful face speaking beautiful words!
Could this be the monster? Don't be absurd.

Monsters live in darkness, right?
Not in the open—not in the light.

How was it supposed to hide—
Without deep shadows to confide?

This being is the most beautiful I have ever seen,
Like the answer to all my wildest dreams.

I am hypnotized by its radiant light—
Guiding me to my heart's delight.

But slowly, like dying winter ice,
Its hands grow cold with death's cruel vice.

The words it spoke grow sour on my tongue.
This is it—my end has just begun.

The realization grows quickly but far too late,
And sadly it has sealed my fate.

Deadly are the desires of the heart.
Deadlier still is the monster who doesn't seem monstrous at the start.

They come as angels as answers to our calls:
Monsters who try to convince us they're not monsters at all.

Foreword

This book is what we need on spiritual warfare. It is so sobering that it also tears down spiritual pride and brings true conviction, it has made me fully aware. Every chapter walks you through different kinds of warfare and gives us the wisdom and knowledge we need in these days in which we live. This book is eye opening from start to finish!

I'm so honored and thankful that Alicia Beattie asked me to write a foreword. This book has ministered to me on so many levels. I didn't want to stop reading because every word just jumped out at me and strengthened and encouraged me. It hits straight to the heart.

Alicia and HelenAnn are God-fearing, mighty women of God filled with much wisdom and knowledge; they are a true product of victory and a wonderful inspiration to everyone. Alicia's and HelenAnn's obedience to the Lord is evident.

Thank you again for allowing the Lord to use you both to deliver such a powerful book.

— Rhoda Faye Diehl
Author and Minister

Introduction

What if we told you that Satan was not the cause of all your problems? What if we told you that you fought past battles you could have avoided?

What if we told you that you possess more power than you realize?

Our free will is a powerful force in our lives, and there are consequences for the things we say and do—despite the fact of our salvation. Obedience is the currency of the kingdom of God. Your obedience determines whether you thrive—or just survive—spiritually. However, on this side of heaven, we are constantly bombarded with "good" things and often confuse them with godly things.

> And no wonder! For even Satan disguises himself as an angel of light. 2 Corinthians 11:14

Satan cannot take away God's promises from us, but he can trick us is into disqualifying ourselves in our walk. God put some very real spiritual laws in place and our ignorance of them can be our destruction. It all comes down to our choices.

Your obedience determines whether you thrive—or just survive—spiritually.

Satan will come disguised as everything we ever thought we wanted, so we need discernment and wisdom to determine whether we are following the angel of light, whose goal is to seduce us and lead us away from God's path. Or are we walking in the true light that dispels the darkness.

Just before the Israelites were to enter the Promised Land, God spoke through Moses, and outlined the blessings of obedience and the curses of disobedience. I will highlight some of Deuteronomy 28, but I encourage you to read this in its entirety on your own.

> Now it shall come to pass, if you diligently obey the voice of the Lord your God, to observe carefully all His commandments which I command you today, that the Lord your God will set you high above all nations of the earth. And all these blessings shall come upon you and overtake you, because you obey the voice of the Lord your God:
>
> "Blessed shall you be in the city, and blessed shall you be in the country.
>
> "Blessed shall be the fruit of your body, the produce of your ground and the increase of your herds, the increase of your cattle and the offspring of your flocks.
>
> "Blessed shall be your basket and your kneading bowl.
>
> "Blessed shall you be when you come in, and blessed shall you be when you go out.
>
> "The Lord will cause your enemies who rise against you to be defeated before your face; they shall come out against you one way and flee before you seven ways." (Deuteronomy 28:1-7 NKJV)
>
> "But it shall come to pass, if you do not obey the voice of the Lord your God, to observe carefully all His commandments and His statutes which I command

you today, that all these curses will come upon you and overtake you:

"Cursed shall you be in the city, and cursed shall you be in the country.

"Cursed shall be your basket and your kneading bowl.

"Cursed shall be the fruit of your body and the produce of your land, the increase of your cattle and the offspring of your flocks.

"Cursed shall you be when you come in, and cursed shall you be when you go out.

"The Lord will send on you cursing, confusion, and rebuke in all that you set your hand to do, until you are destroyed and until you perish quickly, because of the wickedness of your doings in which you have forsaken Me." (Deuteronomy 28:15-20 NKJV)

We all understand that we are under grace today, and no longer living under the burden of the Law of Moses, but Jesus came to fulfil the law. That means these principles still apply and were not nullified by the cross. If they had been, Ananias and Sapphira would not have perished after they lied to Peter.

But a certain man named Ananias, with Sapphira his wife, sold a possession. And he kept back part of the proceeds, his wife also being aware of it, and brought a certain part and laid it at the apostles' feet. But Peter said, "Ananias, why has Satan filled your heart *to lie to the Holy Spirit* and keep back part of the price of the land for yourself? While it remained, was it not your own? And after it was sold, was it not in your own control?

Why have you conceived this thing in your heart? You have not lied to men but to God."

Then Ananias, hearing these words, fell down and breathed his last. So great fear came upon all those who heard these things

Now it was about three hours later when his wife came in, not knowing what had happened. And Peter answered her, "Tell me whether you sold the land for so much?"

She said, "Yes, for so much."

Then Peter said to her, "How is it that you have agreed together to test the Spirit of the Lord? Look, the feet of those who have buried your husband are at the door, and they will carry you out." Then immediately she fell down at his feet and breathed her last. And the young men came in and found her dead, and carrying her out, buried her by her husband. (Acts 5:1-5, 7-10 NKJV, emphases mine)

Satan tempted Ananias and Sapphira to lie. They let the Enemy into their hearts with the root of greed—and they paid the consequences. Instead of falling on their knees in repentance, they stood by their sin. They thought they were smart enough to fool God. They had a choice, and they made the wrong one.

It all comes down to our choices: What you do matters. What you say matters. What you don't do and don't say—matters. We all fall short every day, but even though we are flawed, there is great hope that we can change. There is much joy in knowing that we do not have to stay trapped in a cycle of toxic behaviors and situations. Through Christ, we can become new people—new creations.

We must let ourselves be as clay in the hands of the Potter. May he mold us, change us, and make something beautiful out of each one of us. May we begin by choosing to be humble and transparent.

> But we are all like an unclean thing,
> And all our righteousnesses are like filthy rags;
> We all fade as a leaf,
> And our iniquities, like the wind,
> Have taken us away
>
> But now, O Lord,
> You are our Father;
> We are the clay, and You our potter;
> And all we are the work of Your hand.
> (Isaiah 64:6,8 NKJV)

It all comes down to this all-important choice that God presents to each one of us: Will we trust him and allow him to form our lives according to his plan, or will we resist his Spirit and walk in the stubbornness of our own hearts, allowing the Enemy to lead us instead? This is our choice.

In these pages, we will explore the spiritual laws that govern God's kingdom and identify some of the "hidden foxes" that can destroy our vineyard. May the Spirit of God guide you in choosing your next move.

Alicia Beattie & HelenAnn Williams Baillie

1

The Truth about Warfare

Spiritual warfare is very real. If we think it isn't, we are making a grave error and doing ourselves an injustice. Warfare is lifelong and ongoing. It occurs for all different reasons in all different seasons, but we are kidding ourselves if we think that just because we are saved, we cannot get attacked. We *need* to engage in the fight, not the opposite. Many people think that because they are a child of God, they do not have to fight, and that evil spirits will not come near them. If that is true, someone should explain that concept to some of the best men in the Bible.

> "I have told you these things, so that in me you may have peace. *In this world you will have trouble.* But take heart! I have overcome the world." (John 16:33 NIV, emphasis mine)

> Behold, I give you the authority to trample on serpents and scorpions, and over all the power of the enemy, and *nothing shall by any means hurt you.* (Luke 10:19 NKJV, emphasis mine)

Both of the statements above are Jesus' teachings. If he thought that once you became born-again you would no longer have to fight, why did he bother to leave these instructions? Why did he give us power and authority over the Enemy if he did not expect us to exercise it? Why did he tell us we would have trouble if that was not the case? The idea that we have been promised an easy life free of conflict is a lie from the pit of hell. Here's the truth: *You are expected to fight!*

The presence of warfare is a good sign.

Just because we are children of God and living a surrendered life, that does not mean we will not be attacked. It does not mean we will not have to stand firm and face things. It does not mean we will not have to deal with demonic spirits that are actively trying to tear us down. All this will happen. This is why we need discernment and wisdom, so that when it does happen, we are ready. David, who knew a lot about warfare, wrote this:

> Blessed be the Lord, my rock who trains my hands for battle and my fingers for warfare. (Psalm 144:1)

God trains our hands for our battles and our fingers for our warfare! The New Testament tells us *we are soldiers of Christ.* Soldiers must fight. That is their purpose and duty. What good soldier does not take a stand, fight, and defend? And remember, good soldiers follow orders.

Often the presence of warfare is a good sign. It's proof that you are moving in the right direction and taking back territory from the Enemy. Did you just think you could waltz right in and take things away from Satan? He has put forth effort to deceive and destroy, and he's certainly not going to give up easily. Satan regards you as just as much of an enemy as you do him. Remember this: Satan's primary mission is to steal, kill and destroy, while ours is to restore, bring life, and resurrect. Since our purposes are diametrically opposed, we are in immediate conflict. When you are taking back what he stole, you are bound to find yourself in a fight.

David was called a man after God's own heart. Such a beautiful distinction! However, that did not mean David was sitting pretty. As a youth, he had to slay Goliath. As he got older, he had to lead many

24

battles, organize mighty men, and then spent years fighting King Saul, the one he had faithfully served and now who sought to kill him for no good reason. Then he had to go with his mighty men and face Goliath's brother. That's a lot of fighting in one lifetime.

The prophet Elijah was heavily steeped in God's anointing and called by God. Elijah fearlessly spoke for God in the war against idolatry. He literally climbed a mountain and called fire down from heaven after soaking an altar with water in his contest against the followers of Baal. After that, he destroyed them. And then there was peace in the land? No. What was the result? *Jezebel, the queen of the nation of Israel, sought to kill him!*

> So, Jezebel sent a messenger to Elijah, saying, "May the gods punish me and do so severely if I don't make your life like the life of one of them by this time tomorrow!" (1 Kings 19:2)

Both David and Elijah were mighty men of God, and yet they still had to fight, and both were attacked. They are just two Old Testament examples (and there are many more), but the same is true of Jesus' disciples. Why do we think that if even they faced opposition that we will not? Yes, even under the new covenant, warfare continued.

2

The Devil's Agenda

Scripture tells us that the Enemy is waiting, roaming like a lion seeking whom he can devour. He is patient in his craftiness, choosing the opportune moment to attack. Sometimes his best strategy is not *how* he attacks but *when*. He can tell when we are at our weakest. In 1 Kings 19, we learn that after receiving Jezebel's message, Elijah was afraid and ran for his life. Why? He was exhausted after fighting a major battle, so it was then that the Enemy came and whispered the lie that sent him running.

Satan loves to come when we are weary, discouraged, exhausted, angry, sad, and overwhelmed. He wants to isolate us from other believers. He wants us to accept his lies as truth. He only has the power we give him though, because we can win and have victory and Satan knows it. Therefore, he does everything he can to prevent us from gaining that ground and that victory.

There is another aspect to his timing, and it is a negative one. We can also experience warfare when we are not obediently operating in the role the Lord has placed us. Doing this opens a door through which the Enemy can attack us, and we can fall into sin.

It happened in the spring of the year, *at the time when kings go out to battle,* that David sent Joab and his servants with him, and all Israel; and they destroyed the people of Ammon and besieged Rabbah. *But David remained at Jerusalem. Then it happened one evening that David arose from his bed and walked on the roof of the king's house.* And from the roof he saw a woman bathing, and the woman was very beautiful to behold. So David sent and inquired about the woman. And someone said, "Is this not Bathsheba, the daughter of Eliam, the wife of Uriah the Hittite?" Then David sent messengers, and took her; and she came to him, and he lay with her, for she was cleansed from her impurity; and she returned to her house. And the woman conceived; so she sent and told David, and said, "I am with child." (2 Samuel 11:1-5 NKJV, emphasis mine)

The fact that he was on the balcony and not the battlefield caused him to fall into adultery and conspire to murder. Satan did not have to do anything to destroy David because David set himself on the path to destruction all on his own. We cannot look pretty and sit comfortably. That is a dangerous place to be. Our position is to fight and engage in battle, not sit on a balcony.

Be sober-minded, be alert. Your adversary the devil is prowling around like a roaring lion, looking for anyone he can devour. Resist him, firm in the faith, knowing that the same kind of sufferings are being experienced by your fellow believers throughout the world. (1 Peter 5:8-9)

These two verses say so much. Let's start with the idea of being sober-minded and alert. To be sober-minded is *to be in control of your mind.* It describes having a sound mind. Your mind is not spinning out of control. Instead, it's sharp, it's focused.

This scripture also says that the devil wants to devour you. To *devour* means to gulp down. Digest that in your mind. The devil wants to fully gulp you down. Some preachers have taught that those lions have no teeth, but the truth is this: The devil wants to destroy you completely. He wants to gulp you down! Teeth or not, his goal is to devour you, and this verse warns us to be alert. We must not let our guard down. Satan doesn't need to try and torment those living in the world, who do not serve God's kingdom. Why? They are not a threat. They are unsaved and living in sin. They are not actively operating in the kingdom of Christ. They are not an adversary. He does not want us advancing God's kingdom. But keep this truth in mind: The deceiving lion is not a match for the Lion of the Tribe of Judah, Jesus Christ.

Growth, change, and building ourselves in the power, love, and truth of the Lord should be a continual process.

Satan has already been defeated and his end is near. He knows it, God knows it, even we know it. Nevertheless, he is still dangerous for us, this is because we let him. We accept his lies as truth; we don't respond to his attacks, but back off instead. Sadder yet, we often give him the opportunities he is seeking. We give him an open door.

This is the scenario far too often: We get saved and we are growing and moving. In time, we get to a point where we feel comfortable. We look at ourselves and say to ourselves, *"Okay then, I am not back there anymore, I have grown leaps and bounds. I am good here. This is enough."* So, we quit building. Since we feel like we are in a good place, we just stay there. Being comfortable leads to complacency. *We are not called to be complacent.* We are called to go and grow and spread his Word. We are a constant work in progress, a construction zone of sorts. Growth, change, and building ourselves in the power, love, and truth of the Lord should be a *continual process.*

> I am sure of this, that he who started a good work in you *will carry it on to completion* until the day of Christ Jesus. (Philippians 1:6, emphasis mine)

This verse speaks to me, it says we will be under construction in one way or another until Jesus comes back. It is also a beautiful promise that what God starts with you he will complete, but we must remember He is a gentleman and will not force us. We must be willing participants. The comfort zone is where growth dies.

> You *were* running a good race. *Who cut in on you to keep you from obeying the truth?* That kind of persuasion *does not come from the one who calls you.* "A little yeast works through the whole batch of dough." I am confident in the Lord that you will take no other view. *The one who is throwing you into confusion,* whoever that may be, *will have to pay the penalty.* Brothers and sisters, if I am still preaching circumcision, why am I still being persecuted? In that case the offense of the cross has been abolished. As for those agitators, I wish they would go the whole way and emasculate themselves! (Galatians 5:7-12 NIV, emphases mine)

This section commends us for running a good race in the past but points out that we are no longer running so well by using past tense: *were* instead of *are*. That means our time of "good running" was in the past and we are now reflecting on it. Where did it go? I love how Paul asks a question next and then follows it with: "That kind of persuasion does not come from the one who calls you."

Sometimes we mix up a toxic form of being comfortable for God's peace and comfort. It is not the same. Peace and true comfort can be found in Christ, despite the most difficult and heartbreaking of circumstances. We can access the peace and comfort of God—no matter what. *Nothing* can remove God's shalom peace from us. However, when being comfortable becomes our focus, we are easily tricked by the Enemy into complacency. That's what happened to David.

> But I fear, lest somehow, as the serpent deceived Eve by his craftiness, so your minds may be corrupted from the simplicity that is in Christ. (2 Corinthians 11:3 NKJV)

And no wonder! For Satan himself transforms himself into an angel of light. (2 Corinthians 11:14 NKJV)

The term "angel of light" is referring to the way the Devil disguises himself as your heart's desire in his effort to divert you or distract you. He does not always come with death threats; sometimes he's sneakier and comes bearing gifts. He'll give you everything he thinks you want. He modeled this behavior when he tempted Jesus in the wilderness, and he will repeat it with you too.

> Then the devil, taking Him up on a high mountain, showed Him all the kingdoms of the world in a moment of time. And the devil said to Him, "All this authority I will give You, and their glory; for this has been delivered to me, and I give it to whomever I wish. Therefore, if You will worship before me, all will be Yours." (Luke 4:5-7 NKJV)

This type of persuasion comes from the pit of hell. *Do not let Satan trick you.* 2 Corinthians 2:11 reminds us that we are not to be ignorant of the Devil's schemes.

Our Lord and Savior speaks and leads us every moment of every day. When we are strictly listening to his voice alone, we leave no room for the Enemy. The Bible says Jesus is the Shepherd, and his sheep know his voice! The concept that God speaks to his people and does not leave them to figure things out on their own is reflected all over the Bible. This is not just a New Testament kind of idea. It's at the heart of our connection with our Lord. We can communicate and we can hear. Jesus said, "My sheep hear my voice, I know them, and they follow me" (John 10:27).

3

The Fruit of Our Sin

L et's revisit that section we read a page or so ago in Galatians 5.

> You *were* running a good race. *Who cut in on you to keep
> you from obeying the truth?* That kind of persuasion
> *does not come from the one who calls you.* "A little
> yeast works through the whole batch of dough." I am
> confident in the Lord that you will take no other view.
> *The one who is throwing you into confusion,* whoever
> that may be, *will have to pay the penalty.* Brothers
> and sisters, if I am still preaching circumcision, why
> am I still being persecuted? In that case the offense of
> the cross has been abolished. As for those agitators,
> I wish they would go the whole way and emasculate
> themselves! (Galatians 5:7-12 NIV, emphases mine)

Yeast represents sin. Paul teaches that just a little sin can have an enormous impact. The *Amplified Version* renders that verse thus: "A little leaven [a slight inclination to error, or a few false teachers] leavens the whole batch [it perverts the concept of faith and misleads the church]." A little sin can do a lot of damage. What does the word *sin* mean? *Missing the mark!* It refers to missing a target when shooting an arrow or throwing a spear. The basic concept is that sin causes our aim to go awry, so that we miss God's mark.

You, my brothers and sisters, were called to be free. *But do not use your freedom to indulge the flesh;* rather, serve one another humbly in love. For the entire law is fulfilled in keeping this one command: "Love your neighbor as yourself." If you bite and devour each other, watch out or you will be destroyed by each other. So I say, walk by the Spirit, *and you will not gratify the desires of the flesh.* For the flesh desires what is contrary to the Spirit, and the Spirit what is contrary to the flesh. They are in conflict with each other, *so that you are not to do whatever you want.* But if you are led by the Spirit, you are not under the law. (Galatians 5:13-18 NIV, emphases mine)

Paul is simply saying that just because you are saved through faith, it does not mean you can take advantage of God's grace. True freedom is not doing whatever we want; on the contrary, doing that makes us a slave to the flesh. True freedom is stripping off the evil, fleshy things of this world and *choosing* to live according to God's original design instead. Our attempts to do this will never be perfect, but this truth will save us from the consequences of the flesh, if we choose to walk in it daily.

Just a little sin can have an enormous impact.

We are warned to not indulge the flesh. Nothing the flesh has is of any use to us. We are called to be free. Where the Spirit of the Lord is, there is freedom, so when we walk by the Spirit and follow the Spirit, the flesh is kept in check as it ought to be. Since the flesh and Spirit are against each other, the more we stay submitted to the Spirit of God and his transforming power, the less we will be distracted and led by the flesh. Jesus is the Way and the Answer!

The acts of the flesh are *obvious:* sexual immorality, impurity and debauchery; idolatry and witchcraft; hatred, discord, jealousy, fits of rage, selfish ambition, dissensions, factions and envy; drunkenness, orgies, and the like. *I warn you, as I did before, that those who live like this will not inherit the kingdom of God.* But the fruit of the Spirit is love, joy, peace, forbearance, kindness, goodness, faithfulness, gentleness and self-control. Against such things there is no law. *Those who belong to Christ Jesus have crucified the flesh with its passions and desires.* Since we live by the Spirit, let us keep in step with the Spirit. Let us not become conceited, provoking and envying each other. (Galatians 5:19-26 NIV, emphases mine)

Note how the fruits of the Spirit are the opposite of the acts of the flesh. That is why they are constantly at war with one another. They are worse than cats and dogs. They are more like oil and vinegar because they do not mix.

We often look at the list of the works of the flesh and think: *Not me! I'm not operating in any of these!* But when you dig inside yourself and break these things down, we will find some of them at work in our lives. There's no getting around it.

What Does Idolatry Look Like Today?

First, let's look at idolatry. Some people think this does not even exist anymore. Nothing could be further from the truth. Idolatry is alive and well. Basically, idolatry means image worship. It's easy to see that in our time. Not only are the false idols of the Bible still around in some cultures, but we have created new, modern-day idols. If you open your eyes to this, it will be easy to see the way image worship is alive and well.

Anything you put above God in your life can be considered an idol. If you spend your free time scrolling social media and neglect time with God, that's an idol in your life. If you practice coping mechanisms to deal with stress instead of praying at all, those mechanisms have become an idol. Prayer should come first. Even good things like work—or your ministry in the body of Christ—can become idols if they are not prioritized correctly. The Enemy will use anything he can to lead us astray. This is why our daily connection to Jesus is so vital.

Maybe you don't follow celebrities (and not everyone does), but we are living in a time in which idol worship is sneaky and very easy to erect in our lives. Anything can become an idol. For some, money and work can be an idol. They get so wrapped up in advancement and keeping up with others, that they neglect their spouses, their families, their community, and of course, God. Our focus is all wrong if we are like this. We become so focused on work and making money that we lose our grasp on what is really important. Money, on its own, is not wrong nor is having a job and working hard. These can be good attributes, but if they come first at the expense of everything else, they may have become idols!

Honestly, one of the biggest idols we may have in our lives is our smartphones! We take them everywhere! Many of us are glued to them continually: watching everything from short videos to full-length movies on them. We even take them to church where, if we aren't careful, we can get caught up in group texts and social media while we're supposed to be listening to a sermon or interacting with the family of God. We use them to take selfies and videos, play games and surf the net. I know I am guilty of wasting screen time on unworthy things before God. This sneaky little idol is powerful. You can see people everywhere staring into them: in traffic at any red light as well as in waiting rooms, malls, restaurants, parks, and anywhere else you can imagine. We have instant access to an endless amount of stuff. My phone tells me at the end of the week how much time I spent on it and what I was doing. If I'm honest, it made me sad the last time I looked at that. I could have spent that time with the Lord, in the Word, in prayer, or with my family. My eyes were opened to how my phone had become an idol.

Sometimes idolatry is even sneakier. If one of the reasons you do not want to go to church or a meeting is because you do not have the right outfit to wear, you have placed your own image over your need to assemble with the family of God. If you spend more time planning outfits and doing your makeup than you do preparing your heart for a word, then that is a clear sign you have idolatry in your life. It is one thing to like to look nice (I'm not saying you should not care about that), but we must make sure our priorities are in the proper order.

Often, it's not superficial things such as looks or outfits. It's the things deep on the inside. It's knowledge and education. There are two types of knowledge, knowledge of this world, and Godly wisdom and knowledge.

> Let no one deceive himself. If anyone among you seems to be wise in this age, let him become a fool that he may become wise. *For the wisdom of this world is foolishness with God.* For it is written, "He catches the wise in their own craftiness"; and again, "The Lord knows the thoughts of the wise, that they are futile." (1 Corinthians 3:18-20 NKJV, emphasis mine)

It is so easy now days to make where we went to university or college the most important focus of our identity. When you walk into offices, it's normal to see someone's diploma on the wall, but why are the walls also full of framed majors and minors and the desks empty of Bibles? Truly, as this verse states, the wisdom of this world is foolishness to God.

It is not bad to know things. The Lord wants us to be intelligent and wise. He does not want us to be dummies. He will graciously give wisdom and understanding if we ask and if we have a reverent fear of him, but that's not the same as prideful knowledge. We need to know where our knowledge comes from, and we need to place it on its proper pedestal at its correct height, and not above that.

> To these four young men God gave knowledge and understanding of all kinds of literature and learning. And

Daniel could understand visions and dreams of all kinds.
(Daniel 1:17 NIV)

In the book of Daniel, the Lord gave these four young men (all were captives in Babylon), the knowledge they needed to excel where they had been placed. However, when push came to shove, they did not trust in their great knowledge as their identity, and they did not place it above the Lord. At the time Israel had been defeated by Babylon and the king wanted only the best young men from the finest families for his palace.

> Then the king instructed Ashpenaz, the master of his eunuchs, to bring some of the children of Israel and some of the king's descendants and some of the nobles, ⁴ young men in whom there was no blemish, but good-looking, *gifted in all wisdom, possessing knowledge* and quick to understand, who had ability to serve in the king's palace, and whom they might teach the language and literature of the Chaldeans. (Daniel 1:3-4 NKJV, emphasis mine)

For them to be selected they had to be smart—full of knowledge and wisdom. Once they arrived at the palace, the Lord gave them even more knowledge and wisdom so they could be the best. In time though they had to choose between their success, knowledge, and comfort—and the Lord. They chose the Lord. They chose not to defile themselves by eating the food and drink of the Babylonians. Instead, they followed the Hebrew law and ate only what was clean.

Later, when the king created a great, golden idol of himself for all the people to worship, these four young men would not bow to that society's idol. When challenged on this point, they answered thus:

> "If that is the case, our God whom we serve is able to deliver us from the burning fiery furnace, and He will deliver us from your hand, O king. But if not, let it be known to you, *O king, that we do not serve your gods,*

*nor will we worship the gold image which you have set
up."* (Daniel 3:17-18 NKJV, emphasis mine)

This is how we should respond to the idols in our lives and the idols
society tries to create for us. We need this boldness. We cannot let our
love for knowledge and education be above the One who gives it. When
we create an idol out of our education and knowledge, it eventually
turns our accomplishments into idols too.

Paul describes a judgment for Christians in 1 Corinthians in which
our deeds will be judged.

> Now if anyone builds on this foundation with gold, silver,
> precious stones, wood, hay, straw, each one's work will
> become clear; for the Day will declare it, because it will
> be revealed by fire; and the fire will test each one's work,
> of what sort it is. If anyone's work which he has built on
> it endures, he will receive a reward. If anyone's work is
> burned, he will suffer loss; but he himself will be saved,
> yet so as through fire. (1 Corinthians 3:12-15 NKJV)

Accomplishments can also be placed on a pedestal above the Lord.
It is not bad to achieve great things, but there is a distinct difference
between the good thing and the godly thing. When we set goals, we
must keep an eternal perspective.

The gold, silver, and precious stones are the godly deeds, done for
the kingdom. They can be big or very small, even every day, mundane
tasks. The wood, hay and straw are the good deeds, but they do not hold
any eternal value because the fire destroys them. Why do we hold such
high regard for achievements that have no value in heaven? And if we
do, how can we place these things above God? What if I told you that a
Sunday School teacher who plants and waters seeds in young children
will earn a greater reward in heaven than the man who became the CEO
of his company by the age of thirty? What if I told you that a couple who
waited until marriage to consummate their love achieved something

greater and will gain a greater reward in heaven over the woman who went to Harvard and became valedictorian. What if I told you that a pastor at a church who helped bring thousands to Christ is richer in heaven than the man who created the electric car and is one of the richest men on earth? When you think about it, we all lead different lives from birth to death dependent on the choices we make and the work we do. Is what we are doing really that important, and is it important enough to make it our identity? If it is all ash and dust in the end, why do we place it above God, the One who created us from the ash and the dust and is forever present?

It's easy to allow these things to take over in our hearts, especially since we live in a society in which the successful and the celebrities are on display like trophies. Their fame and fairy-tale lives are tied to what they have achieved so far, but in reviewing their achievements, we should take a hard look at their lives. When you examine them apart from all the glitz and glam, who are they? Half of them go through multiple divorces; some of them are on drugs; others suffer from severe mental illness. For most of them, nothing they say or do points to Jesus. On top of that, the loneliness and heartache associated with fame is extremely daunting. Why would we want any part of that?

And yet, we sometimes subconsciously try to be like our favorite celebrity. Way too often, we teach our children how to imitate them too. We think: *If my son or daughter goes to this school and gets this job, he or she will be as successful as that famous lawyer. If I buy my daughter these outfits and take her to these places and make her attend these parties in this city, it's possible that she could get picked up like that famous model. If I make my son play this sport and attend this college and make him train hard, he will be a pro like that famous player.*

We should be teaching them to imitate Christ. How do we do that? If we are modeling our lives after Christ, we are modeling that same behavior to our children. And believe me, our kids get the message about what is important and what is not from a young age.

Even though it's counterculture, we need to point to Christ in our choices. And we need to do that with wisdom, understanding, and humility.

What Does the Bible Mean by Witchcraft?

Next on that list is witchcraft. I know, I know, you might think no one would dare practice witchcraft in today's day and age, but I tell you it is alive and well. It is even operating in the church. You may not be in a coven and casting spells, but that is not all that defines witchcraft.

Witchcraft refers to manipulation, deception, mind games, and much more. When you speak ill of someone, that's witchcraft. Think of how Satan, the serpent, deceived Eve. He used witchcraft. He manipulated, lied, and played mind games to deceive Eve. Stop and let this sink in: *Satan is the father of lies and when he speaks a lie, he is speaking his native language*, so *what language are you speaking when you lie, manipulate, and play mind games with others?* Not a heavenly one!

If you look up the word translated as *witchcraft* from Galatians 5 in Strong's concordance, it is *pharmakeia* in the Greek. It refers to the use of medicine, drugs, or spells, magic, sorcery, and enchantment.[1] This is a lesson in itself, but it also connects to selling or giving other people drugs. In fact, you can see the word "pharmacy" in that word.

There's no question that the next one on the list is rampant. Simple plain old jealousy is beyond alive and well. It's widespread. People get on social media, full of their hate and jealousy of another, and vomit all over the page. Others have seemingly perfect lives but are driven by comparison with material things. Their world is so petty that they'll hate somebody else out of jealousy. If we are always thinking about how another person has a nicer car and house then we do, that's straight flesh.

1. James Strong, "Pharmakeia," Strong's Greek: 5331. φαρμακεία (pharmakeia) -- the use of medicine, drugs or spells (Biblehub), accessed May 30, 2022, https://biblehub.com/greek/5331.htm.

Take a few moments and go back and look at that list again. Are there any areas that particularly hit home for you? Is your life in good order according to the will and calling of God? How do you know that?

There is no shame in asking God to show us where we need to change. The last thing we want, as his followers, is to let weeds grow up in the soil of our hearts and minds. It's very easy to get caught up in the world we live in, in which mainstream media tells us half-truths or flat-out lies to manipulate us into believing their narrative as opposed to the whole truth. It seems like we are surrounded by this wherever we look, but we must ask ourselves this: What seeds are we sowing? What thoughts are we letting take root in our minds? If we are not careful, we will let weeds grow where flowers should be blooming, that will produce fruit.

Here's a quick fruit checklist that can help you assess yourself.

Fruit of Sin

Sexual immorality
Impurity
Debauchery
Idolatry
Witchcraft
Hatred
Discord
Jealousy and fits of rage
Selfish ambition
Dissensions and factions
Envy
Drunkenness

Fruit of the Spirit

Love
Joy
Peace
Forbearance

Kindness
Gentleness
Self-control
Goodness
Faithfulness

Are there moments in your life when you try to bend people to your will by telling half-truths? Even if your point is wrong?

Do you tell stories that have added spice to them for the purpose of framing someone else?

Is there a problem you want to avoid that you make excuses for?

We all do these things. We fall short, but it's these small white lies that get us speaking in an unholy language, leaving the door wide open for the Enemy to sneak in.

Remembering that we are all works in progress, check any area in which you have an issue. Ask the Holy Spirit to guide you and show you. Please remember that there is no condemnation in Christ. We are all working on areas in our lives and growing. God convicts and helps us, while the Enemy condemns us and tells us we are hopeless. God is purifying us, and we can trust him in that process.

Next, go ahead and circle any area in which you are doing well. We all have strengths and weaknesses. Allowing the Spirit to guide us in our heart assessment allows us to grow and mature in areas where we are weaker and appreciate our growth at the same time. Keep this list and come back to it whenever you want a checkup. Since we are always changing, I enjoy coming back to my lists and seeing how far the Lord has brought me.

4

The Importance of Purity

When we operate in the works of the flesh, it makes cracks in our walls, and chinks in our armor. These gaps give the Enemy opportunity to come in. He does not always need you to leave a door open; he will take any space you give him. The Enemy (and his minions) like dirt. They thrive in dirt. That's why they love it when we allow unclean things (the dirt of the flesh and this world) into our lives and homes. Think about it. The story of Legion in Mark 5 started with an unclean spirit. Unclean spirits are not operating in clean lives, in refined lives, in lives surrendered to God's will and ways. Unclean spirits gain access through the dirt in someone's life—the dirt that the person has not bothered to clean up. Sometimes attacks can be partially self-inflicted.

Unclean spirits gain access through the dirt in someone's life

My pastor said this: "The gifts of the Spirit don't change our character, but the fruit of the Spirit does." We must deal with our flesh and crucify it daily. We must actively cast away its desires and submit to the process of changing and growing, so we bear good fruit. If you really examine this fruit, you will see they reflect the character of Christ. Let's review them.

> But the fruit of the Spirit is love, joy, peace, patience, kindness, goodness, faithfulness, gentleness, and self-control. The law is not against such things. (Galatians 5:22-23)

For the fruit of the Spirit to grow unhindered requires our participation with the Spirit of God within us. That means it is possible to grow them by crucifying the flesh and putting on the armor of God each and every day—in the same way you brush your teeth every day.

> Therefore, I say this and testify in the Lord: You should no longer walk as the Gentiles do, in the futility of their thoughts. They are darkened in their understanding, excluded from the life of God, because of the ignorance that is in them and because of the hardness of their hearts. They became callous and gave themselves over to promiscuity for the practice of every kind of impurity with a desire for more and more. But that is not how you came to know Christ, assuming you heard about him and were taught by him, as the truth is in Jesus, to take off your former way of life, the old self that is corrupted by deceitful desires, to be renewed in the spirit of your minds, and to put on the new self, the one created according to God's likeness in righteousness and purity of the truth. Therefore, putting away lying, speak the truth, each one to his neighbor, because we are members of one another. Be angry and do not sin. Don't let the sun go down on your anger, and don't give the devil an opportunity. Let the thief no longer steal. Instead, he is to do honest work with his own hands, so that he has something to share with anyone in need. No foul language should come from your mouth, but only what is good for building up someone in need, so that it gives grace to those who hear. And don't grieve God's Holy Spirit. You were sealed by him for the day of redemption. Let all bitterness, anger

and wrath, shouting and slander be removed from you, along with all malice. And be kind and compassionate to one another, forgiving one another, just as God also forgave you in Christ. (Ephesians 4:17-32)

This passage outlines many of our problems: lying (not even those little white lies are okay), dealing with anger, and foul language are a few that are mentioned. We hear bad language nearly everywhere these days: on the TV, in conversation, and in the lyrics on the radio. Everyone has words that trip them up more than others. Too often we think that if we are angry, it's okay to use them too. We allow ourselves to act out and let it rip. We justify our anger and our responses. If someone messes with my kid, that person has got to deal with Momma and Daddy Bear. We tend to think certain situations justify our actions and the subsequent use of bad language that goes with it. However, the Bible warns us repeatedly about anger and its dangers. This same passage urges us not to let the day end in anger; and note what follows that statement: Do not give the Devil an opportunity. That's pretty much all he is looking for: an opportunity; other translations say a foothold. Walking in unforgiveness is another big way we allow the Enemy space, as the Bible says.

Anyone you forgive, I do too. For what I have forgiven— if I have forgiven anything—it is for your benefit in the presence of Christ, so that we may not be taken advantage of by Satan. For we are not ignorant of his schemes. (2 Corinthians 2:10-11)

Giving him a foothold reminds me of a scene from a television show: There's a knock at the door. As the person answers it, they look out the peephole and put the little chain on its hook. But as they open the door, they realize it's a bad person. As they try to close it, the intruder sticks his boot in the small gap that the chain allowed and forces the door. All he needed was that little opening, that little opportunity. That's all the Enemy of our faith needs too—a small opportunity, a foothold; and he will try to kick your door wide open too.

> Therefore, be imitators of God, as dearly loved children, and walk in love, as Christ also loved us and gave himself for us, a sacrificial and fragrant offering to God. But sexual immorality and any impurity or greed should not even be heard of among you, as is proper for saints. Obscene and foolish talking or crude joking are not suitable, but rather giving thanks. For know and recognize this: Every sexually immoral or impure or greedy person, who is an idolater, does not have an inheritance in the kingdom of Christ and of God. (Ephesians 5:1-5)

The first step to cleansing our lives is looking at these "works of the flesh" and intentionally beginning to remove them. We need to see how they are operating in our lives. When these issues are left unchecked, they not only leave us open for attack, but also clog the flow of the anointing in our lives. If we got in a shower, we would not want a half-clogged stream of water to wash our hair, so why would we want a stopped-up flow in our spiritual lives?

Earlier we looked at what the word sin actually means, it was to miss the mark. What do you do when you miss the mark? You get up, dust yourself off, *take aim*, and try again. You practice until you hit the target. You are going to miss that mark! Everyone does. You are human. The important part is to get up and practice until you succeed. Then you move on to the next target. This is a process that we repeat as often as necessary.

So, sin means to miss the mark, and we are told to repent when we sin. Even though we have heard the term *repent* our whole lives, I think many of us do not understand its real meaning. We get that term from the Greek word *metanoeo*, which means a change of mind, repentance, and conversion.[2] It is a call to turn or change one's attitude and ways. Author Rick Renner said, "It's a decision to completely change or to

---

2. James Strong, "3340 Metanoeó," Strong's Greek: 3340. μετανοέω (metanoeó) -- to change one's mind or purpose, accessed May 30, 2022, https://biblehub.com/greek/3340.htm.

entirely turn around in the way one is thinking, believing, or living."[3] We need to clean out our spiritual house and lives. This includes our minds and mouths too. Doing this will close the door on the Enemy. It is time to give him an eviction notice in Jesus' name.

There is only one way to make these changes: with Jesus' help. I encourage you to meditate on this verse and learn what it truly means to transform your mind.

> Don't copy the behavior and customs of this world, *but let God transform you into a new person by changing the way you think.* Then you will learn to know God's will for you, which is good and pleasing and perfect. (Romans 12:2 NLT, emphasis mine)

You can become a new person; you do not have to be stuck. Everyone has things about themselves that they do not like, but we have this hope:

We can change. I can change. You can change. Not of our own power and might, but through Christ Jesus who makes all things new!

3. Rick Renner, Sparkling Gems from the Greek: 365 New Gems to Equip and Empower You for Victory Every Day of the Year (Tulsa, OK: Institute Books, 2016).

5

Our Choice

B efore we move on, I want to point out that the works of the flesh we've been studying so far are not just ideas in our head. These weeds end up manifesting themselves in our lives through our actions and deeds. For instance, most people do not jump quickly from being married to having an affair. That affair began with a hidden sin and grew into the affair. That is why it is important to recognize and root out seemingly small issues before they get deeply rooted and bear fruit. Infidelity can have many roots, but it can't happen if those roots are pulled.

Some of our problems can be chalked up to our own bad decisions and unwise choices which we made with our own free will.

I also want us to recognize that although we have a very real enemy with a host of evil spirits in his ranks, and while witchcraft and sorcery are more real than we realize, they are not responsible for everything bad that happens in our lives. Sometimes we are under demonic attack, but not all the time. As believers we often give Satan credit for what goes wrong in our lives. We say things like: "It's the Enemy's fault that this happened or that happened." We blame him for everything, but continue to operate in, and feed, our flesh. This opens doors to bad places and bad spaces. When we open the door for the Enemy to have a field day, we can no longer pin the whole thing on him. God gave us all free will, and the truth is that some of our problems can be chalked up to our own bad decisions and unwise choices which we made with our own free will. Our choices to feed our flesh will bear the fruit of the flesh. Let's review these verses:

> Now the *works of the flesh* are obvious: sexual immorality, moral impurity, promiscuity, idolatry, sorcery, hatreds, strife, jealousy, outbursts of anger, selfish ambitions, dissensions, factions, envy, drunkenness, carousing, and anything similar. I am warning you about these things—as I warned you before—that those who practice such things will not inherit the kingdom of God. (Galatians 5:19-21, emphasis mine)

> Therefore, putting away lying, speak the truth, each one to his neighbor, because we are members of one another. Be angry and do not sin. Don't let the sun go down on your anger, *and don't give the devil an opportunity.* Let the thief no longer steal. Instead, he is to do honest work with his own hands, so that he has something to share with anyone in need. No foul language should come from your mouth, but only what is good for building up someone in need, so that it gives grace to those who hear. And don't grieve God's Holy Spirit. You were sealed by him for the day of redemption. Let all bitterness, anger and wrath, shouting and slander be removed from you, along with all malice. And be kind and compassionate to one another, forgiving one another, just as God also forgave you in Christ. (Ephesians 4:25-32, emphasis mine)

We are warned not to give the devil an opportunity. You see, that is all he needs—just a small opening. As an opportunistic being, the Devil is ready and willing to walk through any door you open.

These portions of Scripture really provide a good checklist of what to watch for, so we can use them to examine ourselves deep within.

God knows we need a standard, and he provided us with a list of what needs to change. If we are operating in the works of the flesh, we are on dangerous ground. We are sinning, and leaving it unchecked, our sin will bear fruit. If we are not sure whether or not we are operating in the flesh, we need to pray for discernment and wisdom, so we can see what needs to be plucked out!

Let's get real with ourselves!

If you think you do not have a problem with anything on that list, please tell me your secret. Why? Because I am a continual work in progress and always working on overcoming my next flaw. *Let's get real with ourselves* and pray to recognize and remove these things.

> If we say that we have no sin, *we deceive ourselves,* and the truth is not in us. (1 John 1:8 NKJV, emphasis mine)

Satan is often called the great deceiver, and he most certainly does not want us to delve into these areas, especially since they give him an open road. This is really our own choice. We are the only ones deceiving ourselves. I encourage you to let the truth of Christ seep into you and allow the Holy Spirit to minister. If you never considered the list in the verses we just read, it's time. Did not Jesus die to set you free from these things? Was Christ's sacrifice in vain? Or are you not applying it correctly? Ask the Lord to remove any scales that might be covering your eyes. He already knows, so do not be ashamed.

> *Yet in all these things we are more than conquerors through Him who loved us.* For I am persuaded that neither death nor life, nor angels nor principalities nor powers, nor things present nor things to come, nor height nor depth, nor any other created thing, shall be able to separate us from the love of God which is in Christ Jesus our Lord. (Romans 8:37-39 NKJV, emphasis mine)

Nothing you have done and no mistake you have made will ever stop God from loving you. In him you are more than a conqueror. He can empower you to make the changes you need to make, so that you can stop leaving doors open for the Enemy to torment you and your loved ones.

What good is it to build a fortress and leave the front gate open and defenseless? Imagine living in a great, big, fortified city with huge walls and watchman on the walls. Picture something out of medieval times. Did they go to the trouble to build all that to protect themselves and their families, and then leave the drawbridge down and the doors and gates wide open, so any enemy could saunter in and destroy them? Sounds silly, doesn't it? Yet we do this spiritually all the time. The devil does not even need to sneak in with a Trojan horse when the gate is wide open for him all the time

I once heard a story of a grandfather who told the tale of two wolves to his grandson. He picked him up and sat him on his knee, creaks echoing from the ancient rocking chair. It was the grandfather's story chair, and all his best stories came when he sat on it. The grandson settled into his grandfather's lap.

"What story is it today, Papa? What dragon do we get to slay today?" asked the little boy as he waved his hand in the air, grasping an imaginary sword and slicing it through the air.

His grandfather grabbed his hand and settled him down before his grandson got to the point where not even a story would tame him. "This is the tale of the two wolves," he answered.

"Humph! That's not about dragons," he said, crossing his arms across his chest. "I wanted a story about a dragon."

His grandfather laughed, "I promise you that these two wolves are more powerful than any dragon!"

Clearing his throat, he continued. "There are two wolves living inside you. One that is good and pure of heart—and the other is evil and seeks destruction. They fight with one another day in and day out—a cycle that never seems to stop."

Confusion draped across the grandson's face as he pulled his lips into a thin line, "But grandfather," he said, "why don't they ever stop fighting? Why do they hate each other? Who wins?"

His grandfather's eyes glossed over as a million memories, good and bad, flashed through his mind all at once. "Well, my boy," he said, pushing the memories back where they belonged: in the past, not here, not in this precious moment with his grandson, "The one you feed is the one that wins."

Whichever one we continually feed will be the one ruling our lives.

The grandfather was speaking of the spirit man and the flesh man inside each of us. Whichever one we continually feed will be the one ruling our lives. Feed the flesh and the flesh will rule; feed the spirit and the spirit will rule. It is a choice that you get to make for yourself.

> Therefore, brethren, we are debtors—not to the flesh, to live according to the flesh. *For if you live according to the flesh you will die;* but if by the Spirit you put to death the deeds of the body, you will live. (Romans 8:12-13 NKJV, emphasis mine)

Have you ever heard the saying that you are what you eat? What have you been eating? Some of us have been eating all the white lies that come our way, and some of us have been the ones telling the white lies. When I was younger, I was never allowed to say the words, "I hate you." When I was about twelve years old, I told one of my younger brothers that I had hated him over something stupid. I got in trouble, of course, because I was mean to my brother, but my dad explained to me how wrong it was to use those words. He explained the weight of that phrase, and it stuck with me. He asked me to consider if that were the last thing I ever said to my brother. What if something happened between now and the next time I saw him? I would have had to live with that mistake for the rest of my life, never being able to go back to fix it. I am twenty-six now, and I have never told anyone, especially my family, that I hated them since. I do not ever want to accidently sow that seed. If I ever did, I would have no one to blame but myself.

Hatred means hostility, and some of us have taken a big bite out of hostility. Hate and hostility are strong words. In fact, the Enemy himself has hostility toward the children of God, so he seeks to destroy us.

Have you ever listened to a conversation and thought, *Wow! She's really hostile?* A related word is contention which means a quarrel. Quarrels seem to be everywhere all the time. You hear arguments in stores, and see them on social media, and even on the highways manifested as road rage. Quarrels are out of control, and we seem to be eating them up. These are just some examples, but the point is that this is evidence of some of the nonsense we are building in our spiritual and physical lives! These practices are of no use to either!

6

Your Wilderness Season

S ister Dianne Olinger recently led a women's meeting about the flow of the Spirit in our lives. She talked about how rivers have great flow and are very refreshing because they continuously flow. Then she pointed out the differences between lakes, that have no flow out, and a river. In the lake, the water looked nasty because of the bacteria and other mucky stuff in it. It was stagnant, and not flowing like a river does. She even talked about dams and how they worked. She got me thinking: If water is clogged and does not flow for any period of time, what happens beyond the blockage? Dry places, dry spaces, and in time deserts and wastelands. Picture a drought-stricken area. A once-flourishing tract of land begins to die. Cracks split the barren land. Wind and erosion remove the good topsoil over time. Nothing grows anymore. We, my friend, are supposed to grow fruit! Fruit does not grow in dead, dry places! A desert represents isolation and separation.

There is a difference between God taking you through a desert wilderness, and going to dwell in one of your own making! The operative word there is "through"; we go through deserts. We don't live *in* them.

Jesus was led into the wilderness by the Spirit and was there for forty days. Christ spent his time fasting and praying and made effective use of his wilderness season. He did not linger there any longer than the ordained time.

The Israelites, on the other hand, wandered in the wilderness for forty years. What could have been a few days (or weeks) journey was prolonged due to their actions and attitudes. They were complainers, ungrateful, and unbelieving. In fact, they are a perfect example on how the works of your flesh can keep you from your promises. Moses was a mighty man of God. He experienced God firsthand, but even he did not get to step foot in the Promised Land because of an act of disobedience.

> And the Lord said to Moses, "You and Aaron must take the staff and assemble the entire community. As the people watch, *speak to the rock over there, and it will pour out its water.* You will provide enough water from the rock to satisfy the whole community and their livestock." So Moses did as he was told. He took the staff from the place where it was kept before the Lord. Then he and Aaron summoned the people to come and gather at the rock. "Listen, you rebels!" he shouted. "Must we bring you water from this rock?" *Then Moses raised his hand and struck the rock twice with the staff, and water gushed out.* So the entire community and their livestock drank their fill. But the Lord said to Moses and Aaron, *"Because you did not trust me enough to demonstrate my holiness to the people of Israel, you will not lead them into the land I am giving them!"* (Numbers 20:7-12 NLT, emphases mine)

God does not show favoritism. If He did, you would think Moses would have been allowed to let this slide. But no. Moses could not (and did not) blame the Devil, the stubborn Israelites he led, or anyone else. He did it himself. He wielded the staff; he struck the rock.

> When Moses had finished giving these instructions to all the people of Israel, he said, "I am now 120 years old, and I am no longer able to lead you. *The Lord has told me, 'You will not cross the Jordan River.'* (Deuteronomy 31:1-2 NLT, emphasis mine)

Then you will die there on the mountain. You will join your ancestors, just as Aaron, your brother, died on Mount Hor and joined his ancestors. *For both of you betrayed me* with the Israelites at the waters of Meribah at Kadesh in the wilderness of Zin. *You failed to demonstrate my holiness* to the people of Israel there. *So you will see the land from a distance, but you may not enter the land* I am giving to the people of Israel." (Deuteronomy 32:50-52 NLT, emphases mine)

You might be thinking this: "But we are under grace. Not the law." That is true. But how many promised lands might your actions have disqualified you from already in your life? Possibly, without you even knowing. We cannot bring our dry desert-based souls with us, and also inherit the promised land God has prepared for us today—full of milk and honey. We must leave all that behind in the desert to die.

Our actions matter.

We may never fully understand why God never allowed Moses to enter the Promised Land but allowed David to remain king after the sin he committed with Bathsheba and Uriah. Perhaps it was the condition of their hearts, God only knows. Nevertheless, this account of Moses in the wilderness should be a sobering reminder of who God is, and that he does not play favorites. Our actions matter.

What we do matters, and we can't blame the Devil for our own choices. We need to start taking accountability for our actions. We say things like, God will bless this mess, but we should consider whether or not the mess could be avoided if we did not choose to act in the flesh. Yes, God will use it for our good in some way but imagine how much better the eternal blessing would be if we were intentionally choosing to walk in the Spirit instead. A battle could be avoided.

However, there is hope for those of us in the wilderness and in the dry places. You are truly never too far gone. Ask the apostle Paul. He had made some very bad choices in his life before his Damascus Road experience, but God brought him to himself, and rerouted his life. We ought never forget that God is a Master Gardener and loves the soil of our hearts. He has plans.

> For the Lord shall comfort Zion: he will comfort all her waste places; and he will make her wilderness like Eden, and her desert like the garden of the Lord; joy and gladness shall be found therein, thanksgiving, and the voice of melody. (Isaiah 51:3 KJV)

Zion has lots of meanings and references in the Bible. One of them means "a parched place." The noun comes from the Hebrew *sayon* which means "dry place" and the verb *sawa* meaning "to be dry."[4] Are we dry today? Are we willing to admit to God that we are in a desert place, a parched place? Are we willing to admit that we have allowed things in our lives that should have been rooted out and are now clogging our flow? Or maybe you have begun rooting things out, but have not replaced them with the things of God: abiding in him, as well as reading your Bible, praying, praising, thanking, and worshipping.

That word *parched* means "deprived of natural moisture"; a parched land is thirsty.[5] So, are you parched today? Are you living in dry places and spaces? If you are, it's okay; there is good news. You do not have to remain in that state any longer!

> The wilderness and the solitary place shall be glad for them; and the desert shall rejoice, and blossom as the rose. (Isaiah 35:1 KJV)

---

4. James Strong, "G4622 - Siōn - Strong's Greek Lexicon (NKJV)," Blue Letter Bible, accessed May 30, 2022, https://www.blueletterbible.org/lexicon/g4622/nkjv/tr/0-1/.

5. "Parched Definition & Meaning," Merriam-Webster (Merriam-Webster), accessed May 30, 2022, https://www.merriam-webster.com/dictionary/parched.

God can make your desert place blossom. You want to see that? Google "desert super blooms" and you'll see how the driest deserts in the world spring up and are covered with beautiful flowers. That is what our God can do. If you want to bloom, he will bloom you right where you are planted, and you will be able to grow with the flow.

> Behold, I will do a new thing; now it shall spring forth; shall ye not know it? I will even make a way in the wilderness, and rivers in the desert. (Isaiah 43:19 KJV)

Even if you are in a wilderness of your making, remember that you serve a God who will make a way in that wilderness. He'll put rivers in your desert. *Is there anyone better than our God!* Let's read that one more time:

> For the Lord shall comfort Zion: he will comfort all her waste places; and he will make her wilderness like Eden, and her desert like the garden of the Lord; joy and gladness shall be found therein, thanksgiving, and the voice of melody. (Isaiah 51:3 KJV)

God does not want you living in a dry, desert wasteland. He has better plans for you and me. If you are parched today, I invite you to start pulling out those roots—the ones that have choked the life out of your bloom. Root them out today right where you are, and He will meet you in that desert and help you bloom.

Your Father invites you to take a drink of his living water. Start closing the door on the Enemy. Start closing the door to sin. Start drinking the living water that flows from the Father. You will not be disappointed. He has a river of living water; and when you start to flow in it, you will see a rose spring up in your wilderness and your rose will turn into a super bloom as you grow. You will be like a great oasis in that desert! In time, there will be no desert. Instead, you will be a thriving garden of the Lord!! He will make a way *if you let him.*

Are you willing today? Are you sick of being dry and parched? Are you thirsty for God? He will pour out on you today if you let him! He is the God that made a cloud the size of a man's hand! He is the God who put dew on fleece! He is the God who cared for Elijah at the brook! Can he do it? Yes! he can!

7

These *Don't* Only Come Out at Night

(The Warnings of 2 Timothy 3, Part 1)

Warfare has many different aspects, levels, and seasons. Sometimes we must deal with demonic forces; sometimes we intercede for others. Sometimes the Enemy attacks, in an effort to stop us from walking in our anointing. But sometimes we are attacked because of little foxes slowly creeping, unnoticed and unchecked, and we know how that ends. They spoil the vine!

> Catch us the foxes, the little foxes that spoil the vines, for our vines have tender grapes. (Song of Solomon 2:15 NKJV)

In context, this was a warning from the Shulamite's brothers to her about allowing anything that might destroy her and Solomon's romance while it was still new. Grapes do not ripen off the vine like bananas do. You could buy green bananas, place them in a paper bag or on a counter for a few days, and in time, have a perfect bunch of yellow bananas. However, if you pluck grapes prematurely, you lose your harvest. There's no saving it.

Note that it says the "little" foxes. Young foxes are sheepish and lack confidence to go out and hunt, so usually their parents bring them food until they can fend for themselves. When they are young, they forage for food like grapes, berries, and bugs. Young foxes cannot reach the tops of the vines where the grapes are, so they chew on the vines, causing them to fall so they can get to the grapes. They will do anything to get those grapes. They will gnaw on the trunk, dig holes around it, and expose the roots. They do more than just steal grapes, they destroy the entire plant.[6] Real foxes are nocturnal, but sin knows no time constraints.

In this text, her brothers delivered a sobering warning to the soon-to-be bride, and it's one we should take seriously ourselves. We must keep the things most precious to us hidden and guarded from the forces that want so desperately to destroy them.

Keep the things most precious to us hidden and guarded.

In this chapter, we will be breaking down sections from 2 Timothy 3. Here they are in their entirety so you can see them in context before we dive into each part. Each section might be quoted again in different translations for the purpose of teaching. The message does not change.

> But know this, that in the last days perilous times will come: For men will be lovers of themselves, lovers of money, boasters, proud, blasphemers, disobedient to parents, unthankful, unholy, unloving, unforgiving, slanderers, without self-control, brutal, despisers of good, traitors, headstrong, haughty, lovers of pleasure rather than lovers of God, having a form of godliness but denying its power. And from such people turn away! *For of this sort are those who creep into households* and make captives of gullible women loaded down with sins, led away by various lusts, always learning and never able to come to the knowledge of the truth. (2 Timothy 3:1-7 NKJV, emphasis mine)

6. Debi Walter, "Beware of These 6 Little Foxes," The Romantic Vineyard (The Romantic Vineyard, July 31, 2013), https://theromanticvineyard.com/2013/07/31/bewareofthese6littlefoxes/amp/.

Last Days and Perilous Times

According to the dictionary, "perilous" means "full of danger or risk, hazardous"[7] and *Strong's Exhaustive Concordance* says the word comes from the Greek *chalepos*, which means "hard (to do or bear)"[8]; and is connected to *kataponeō* which means "to oppress."[9]

What you need to understand before we go any further is this: The days are winding down. We only need to look at the world and know God's Word to see that. Warfare is going to get harder and trickier. The Enemy is going to try and stop us. This world is going to get increasingly evil. It's going to be dangerous, and he is looking to oppress us. We need to begin to open our eyes and allow God to change us and forge us, so we are prepared.

Warfare is going to get harder and trickier.

Let's stop for a minute and pray about this together:

Lord, we come to You this day with thanksgiving for who You are. Before we go any further, I just want to thank You and praise You for all that You have done for us already. You have overpaid us in more ways than one. I pray that we will open our hearts and our minds to You right now. That we would be good soil for the seed (Your Word) to fall in. Please fertilize the soil of our hearts, so that we can produce good fruit. I pray we won't just receive it, but we would let it take root and change us. May it spread within us and give us a harvest of change and growth. I rebuke the bird of the air that would come

7. "Perilous Definition & Meaning," Merriam-Webster (Merriam-Webster), accessed May 30, 2022, https://www.merriam-webster.com/dictionary/perilous.

8. James Strong, "G5467 - Chalepos - Strong's Greek Lexicon (KJV)," Blue Letter Bible, accessed May 30, 2022, https://www.blueletterbible.org/lexicon/g5467/kjv/tr/0-1/.

9. James Strong, "G2669 - Kataponeō - Strong's Greek Lexicon (KJV)," Blue Letter Bible, accessed May 30, 2022, https://www.blueletterbible.org/lexicon/g2669/kjv/tr/0-1/.

to steal it. I pray we would allow You to cultivate us for good fruit to grow and that we would allow You to change and refine us with Your refiner's fire. Help us take the knowledge in our heads and move it to our hearts, so that we can be both knowers and doers of Your Word. In Jesus' name we pray. Amen.

But the [Holy] Spirit explicitly and unmistakably declares that in later times some will turn away from the faith, paying attention instead to deceitful and seductive spirits and doctrines of demons. (1 Timothy 4:1 AMP)

Deceiving (Seductive) Spirits and Doctrines of Demons

Now days we can easily look around and identify these spirits in action. They constantly come after us and try to seduce us to sin and practice the ways of the world. They try to deceive us to embrace false doctrines through the power of deception.

My young niece often asks me questions about why God tells us not to do some things, even though they seem harmless, even fun. I explain that even though a poison dart frog is beautiful, it's deadly. Its colors are bold and extravagant but touching that beautiful frog would kill you within minutes of your interaction with it. Seductive and deceiving spirits work the same way. They paint death up beautifully and sell it to you with lies of future fulfillment and satisfaction.

For a time is coming when people will no longer listen to sound and wholesome teaching. They will follow their own desires and will look for teachers who will tell them whatever their itching ears want to hear. They will reject the truth and chase after myths. (2 Timothy 4:3-4 NLT)

We have preachers today that tell us we don't need to repent. That is a deception. We *must* repent. It is a vital part of our Christian walk. After helping and healing a few people, Jesus said, "Go and sin no more." That's a command to repentance. Repentance actually protects us.

About a year ago, a well-known minister that many followed started posting misleading information on social media. He began teaching that we should just go to Jesus, but that repentance wasn't necessary. That one small post influenced countless people to believe that repentance didn't matter, and there were no consequences for sin.

We must be alert for these false doctrines, false teachers, and anyone who would mislead the children of God. We must be wise watchman and make sure our lives are full of God's truth and his Spirit, so that our families know the truth, and we are not misled.

Dear friends, do not believe everyone who claims to speak by the Spirit. You must test them to see if the spirit they have comes from God. For there are many false prophets in the world. (1 John 4:1 NLT)

We must test the spirits. When we do this, we can not only point our kids and grandkids in the right direction, but also the outside world. We, as believers, should always point to Jesus. We don't want to point to this world.

Deceptive spirits can work through close friends and family too, so we must be vigilant. We are all broken people in need of a Savior, and sadly the Enemy can activate the people closest to us in their brokenness to try to make us stumble. It is a war tactic. I'm not saying they are possessed, but it's those open doors. Open doors allow oppression, and that oppression gives the Enemy a foothold to use them against you.

Now don't get me wrong, they probably have no clue that they are seducing and deceiving you into doing something wrong, but it can happen. If you aren't wise you will fall into the trap. It can be as simple as this scenario:

Cousin: Hey, want to go take the kids to the haunted house?

You: No, I can't. I'm sorry. I'm not allowed.

Cousin: Says who?

You: My pastor does.

Cousin: Why is that? I don't see the big deal.

You: It's evil and promotes fear and evil spirits.

Cousin: No, it doesn't! Who told you that? It's just fun. They are sooo corny. Please just come with me. I won't tell anyone, and we won't post any pictures.

You: I don't know.

Cousin: Please, just come. Be fun again. You don't need to be so boring.

Just like that the trap is set, and if we aren't on guard, we will fall into it and that's just one example, and a small one at that. We need to be alert and test the spirits. If it's not the Holy Spirit, then it's not a spirit we should be entertaining.

Lovers of Self

> People will be lovers of themselves, lovers of money, boastful, proud, abusive, disobedient to their parents, ungrateful, unholy. (2 Timothy 3:2 NIV)

This is often thought of as pride, but it's more than that. A lover of self is a person that only considers themselves. They have a wholly selfish mindset. Large or small, if it does not benefit them in some way, they are not interested. We are not called to be self-centered and self-focused, but God-centered and God-focused. I can't help but think of JFK's inaugural address in 1961, and his now-famous words: "Ask not what your country can do for you, but what you can do for your country." Spiritually I render this quote like this: Ask not what God is going to do for you, but instead ask God what you can do for him! What can we do for his kingdom?

"I am the vine, you are the branches. He who abides in Me, and I in him, bears much fruit; for without Me you can do nothing." (John 15:5 NKJV)

We are not the vine, and God is not the branches. At times, it seems that we get that mixed up. By making ourselves the vine, we create a self-centered worldview. We need to remember our place.

If anyone does not abide in Me, he is cast out as a branch and is withered; and they gather them and throw them into the fire, and they are burned. If you abide in Me, and My words abide in you, you will ask what you desire, and it shall be done for you. By this My Father is glorified, that you bear much fruit; so you will be My disciples. (John 15:6-8 NKJV)

Once again, we are not the vine. If we, as branches, try to take the place of The Vine, we will fail. We will be cast out. We will wither. The little foxes can spoil vines, but not *THE* Vine. We need to abide in his vine, not try to create our own. Life flows from his. If we let the fox of self-love creep in, it can destroy our tender grapes. But in him, we can bear much fruit.

Lovers of Money

I hate how this world teaches perverted gospels. Either Jesus wants us to be poor and starving, or we can speak a twenty-room mansion into our life in a day. They think we will either starve or be immensely prosperous. But God never tells us that we cannot have money. He tells us not to love money and be greedy. Scripture says it like this:

For *the love* of money is a root of all kinds of evil, for which some have strayed from the faith in their *greediness*, and *pierced themselves* through with many sorrows. (1 Timothy 6:10 NKJV, emphases mine)

Don't love money more than people, God, or the church! Don't be greedy. It says they pierce themselves. This is self-inflicted. Why pierce yourself with the sorrows of greed when Jesus was pierced so you could have freedom from those sorrows?

> *But He was pierced* for our offenses, He was crushed for our wrongdoings; the punishment for our well-being was laid upon Him, and by His wounds we are healed. (Isaiah 53:5 NASB, emphasis mine)

In the book of Malachi, the Lord spoke to his people about this. At the time, they were fearful and unfaithful to God and his covenants, while in the same breath blaming God for being unfaithful because they were suffering. Sound familiar? They were leaving footholds for the enemy by not offering proper sacrifices and not honoring the covenant of marriage: the priests were cheating on their wives and some of them were marrying pagan women. They were not being obedient. The Lord commanded them to tithe properly to set them back on the right path again.

> "Will a man rob God? Yet you have robbed Me! But you say, 'In what way have we robbed You?' *In tithes and offerings.* You are cursed with a curse, for you have robbed Me, even this whole nation. Bring all the tithes into the storehouse, that there may be food in My house, *And try Me now in this,* " says the Lord of hosts, "If I will not open for you the windows of heaven and pour out for you such blessing that there will not be room enough to   receive it. "And I will rebuke the devourer for your sakes, so that he will not destroy the fruit of your ground, *nor shall the vine fail to bear fruit for you in the field,* " says the Lord of hosts; "And all nations will call you blessed, for you will be a delightful land," says the Lord of hosts. (Malachi 3:8-12 NKJV, emphases mine)

Money and wealth are powerful forces and what we do with them reflects our hearts. Jesus said this:

For where your treasure is, there your heart will be also (Matthew 6:21 NKJV).

God commanded the people to tithe because he wanted them to set their treasures right and realign their hearts with him. Our actions either enable us to be more holy or root us more deeply in the things of this world. We tithe to show that money does not own us. We own it and we choose to honor the one who gave it to us in the first place. He wants us to sow into a ministry, regardless of how much our tithe may be. There are many great ministries and causes; just pick one. Test the Lord in this. We grasp tightly to our money because we are afraid of losing it. Place it in the care of the one who gave it to you and set your heart right with the Lord. Realign your desires with his, and watch how he blesses you, as you begin to loosen your grip on this world and grasp his kingdom.

When you are obedient to this command, he promises to rebuke the Devourer and protect the fruit of the vine, so we should not allow the little foxes of greed and the love of money to creep in and eat the grapes before they have ripened.

Boasters

These are grumblers, complainers, walking according to their own lusts; and they mouth great swelling words, flattering people to gain advantage. (Jude 1:16 NKJV)

These are sensual persons, who cause divisions, not having the Spirit. (Jude 1:19 NKJV)

Jesus taught that a kingdom divided against itself cannot stand. Therefore, it is dangerous to complain and grumble, that causes divisions. In order for the kingdom of God to advance, there must be unity.

How many times a week do we grumble and complain? Even about the things we pray about, like our children, husbands, and church?

When my sister-in-law was expecting my niece, the baby was diagnosed with a horrible heart condition. The doctors told us the worst and told us to expect the worst. That she was not going to make it. And if she somehow did make it full term, she would only survive a few months. January rolled around and my niece was born, and God gave her a miracle that brings tears to my eyes, to this day and will for the rest of my life. Hours after she was born, her body started to fail, and she had to be put on a ventilator and life support. We did not get to hear her newborn cry, the very thing most people complain about in the middle of the night. The doctors told us that the ventilator might damage her vocal cords and we might never get to hear her sweet little voice ever. We would watch her cry, but it was silent. She was scheduled to have open heart surgery when she was eleven days old and another surgery a week later. The second surgery only had a twenty percent survival rate.

During her first surgery, the doctors watched a miracle take place: When they connected the parts they were supposed to connect, they watched as her heart began to pump and beat like a normal healthy heart despite its underdevelopment. Because of this, that second deadly surgery was no longer needed. God continued to amaze us when her single kidney grew to be large enough to cover the work of two. Because she had two anatomical problems (in her heart and liver), the doctors said she would have birth defects, such as autism or Down's syndrome, but as she got older, none of that happened. When they took her off the ventilator, none of us were ever more happy to hear a baby's cry.

Today she is a perfectly healthy two-year-old. The only evidence of those harsh beginnings is the faint scar on her chest. She runs, she's rough, and she's at the stage when she asks a million questions and does not shut up. It's in those moments when I allowed the miracle to become mundane that I start to complain about the voice I prayed we wouldn't lose.

We cannot allow our blessings and miracles to become the source of our complaints. Our complaints allow the Enemy legal access to us and those blessings. We need to keep a sober mind about what it means to be thankful instead of choosing to be spoiled and ungrateful. If those blessings were ever in danger, we would be on our knees begging God for another miracle, regretting all the time we spent complaining about them and wishing we could turn back time and show our gratitude and love again.

That verse we read earlier in Jude also says they walked according to their own lusts, or in other words, their own desires. Here's a sad truth: Too many of us go to church to get a word, or seek a miracle, or get to a prophet to ask what God says (like we can't hear from him ourselves). This is a form of living according to our desires. How? Church is centered on worshiping God, and God's prophets and prophecy flow in the Spirit of God when he wills it, not when we desire it. The church experience is about seeking him and entering his presence. It's not focused on what we can gain. We should not be looking for signs and wonders. We should follow him for himself, and let the signs and wonders be the bonus if they come.

If we seek him just for his signs, we risk not knowing him.

This is what Jesus was pointing out when he said this: "Unless you people see signs and wonders, you will by no means believe" (John 4:48, NKJV). There's a deep sense of disappointment in Jesus' tone in this statement. We need to take heed because if we seek him just for his signs, we risk not knowing him, but only knowing *about* him. That will produce a nominal, superficial relationship—not a saving one.

Jesus also said, "For false christs and false prophets will rise and show great signs and wonders to deceive, if possible, even the elect" (Matthew 24:24, NKJV). Therefore, it is dangerous to focus on our own desires and seek signs and wonders as the foundation of our faith. On top of not building a strong relational foundation, it leaves a foothold for deception. The spirit of false teachers can also perform signs and wonders; and if we do not have a solid foundation of faith, we will be taken captive and led astray.

> And many of the Samaritans of that city believed in Him because of the word of the woman who testified, "He told me all that I ever did." So when the Samaritans had come to Him, they urged Him to stay with them; and He stayed there two days. And many more believed because of his own word. Then they said to the woman, "Now we believe, not because of what you said, for we ourselves have heard Him and we know that this is indeed the Christ, the Savior of the world." (John 4:39-42 NKJV)

Jesus did not turn the water into wine for the woman at the well. Instead, he gently called her out on her sin. He spoke this deep truth: that he was the living water, and nothing else in this world would satisfy her. She as well as many Samaritans took him at his word. That's all they needed. And that is all we need too. There is a place for signs, wonders, and miracles, but they come as happy additions to abiding in him. Our focus should be on what he desires for us, not what we desire for ourselves.

Here is a good indicator whether you are living according to your own desires or not. If you are more interested in vacations, sports, entertainment, and shopping than you are in the things of God and church, you need to check your heart. Pray this prayer to reveal the condition of the desires of your heart:

> *Father, help me. Guide me and show me anything that is not of you. Reveal to me any areas in which I am out of balance or misaligned. I know that through you, I can grow, mature, and be a better ambassador. Help me to see how your will is always better than what the world offers. Make my heart clean; renew my spirit. Help my*

crooked path become straight. Remove anything from my heart and life that should not be there and help me replace it with the things of you. In your name I pray. Amen.

The truth is that God wants to give us the desires of our hearts: the God-given desires he planned for us when he was forming us in our mother's womb—not the desires the world has thrust upon us. The world's plans will lead us astray and leave room for evil to gain access. On the flip side, God's desires bring joy and personal satisfaction. David wrote this: "Create in me a clean heart, O God, and renew a steadfast spirit within me (Psalm 51:10 NKJV).

8

Zip Thy Lip!

(The Warnings of 2 Timothy 3, Part 2)

Proud

He is proud, knowing nothing, but is obsessed with disputes and arguments over words, from which come envy, strife, reviling, evil suspicions. (1 Timothy 6:4 NKJV)

A proud person is in reality an ignorant person. They truly know nothing. They may think they know it all, but they don't. It's just a façade. Even if they claim to be believers, if they are walking in pride, their minds are blinded. Although they may be reading the Bible, their pride is the fox that spoils the vine and does not allow the Word to produce fruit in their lives. Their pride blocks them.

These people love disputes. We all know that one person that always ends up in disputes. They'll argue anything and everything with anyone, even if they don't know anything about the topic. True soap-opera drama follows them everywhere they go. It's easy to get embroiled in these conversations and their peripheral troubles if we are not on our guard. If you don't know someone like that, just take care not to *be* that person.

1 Timothy says the proud have "evil suspicions." Those that see evil suspicion in others are often the ones guilty of this themselves. It makes me think of a person that does something for all the right reasons, but

another sees evil intent in their actions. This is evil suspicion. It might sound something like this: "Oh them? They aren't really doing that for the right reason. They just want you to think they love Jesus."

This is also called *projecting*. A proud person often projects *their* faults and shortcomings onto other people and accuses them of the behaviors they themselves are doing. As they do this, they might be playing victim or claiming how good they are. They do not know how to accept the fact that some people have genuine true hearts because they do not have one, so they do not understand it.

If this is you, I urge you to consider your ways and allow this truth to convict you and bring you to repentance. This is a dangerous way to live. You are allowing the Enemy to use you as a weapon, destroying yourself and everyone around you. Over time, this will destroy your relationships with people in and out of the church.

The scariest thing about the proud spirit is found at the end of the verse. The Word says they are deprived of the truth. We know Jesus is the Truth Incarnate and we know where to find his message: God's Word! It says they imagine godliness is a way to material gain. This is a sad statement. We do not gain materially from doing God's work. This is prosperity teaching at its finest (or worst depending on your point of view). When we serve and surrender to God, our greatest gain is knowing him and eternal salvation, not in getting stuff. The more time you spend in his presence and his truth, the less you desire what the world has to offer, and the more you yearn for the spiritual things of God.

Disobedient to Parents

In today's culture, kids aren't just talking back; there is an all-time high in disobedience and the spirit of rebellion. I have seen videos of kids crying how they hate their parents because of their voting choices! There are even those hating their parents for letting them be born into white privilege. We must build our kids on the firm foundation of God.

We must make sure they are rooted in the things of Christ, not the non-sense of this world.

> Honor your father and your mother, *that your days may be long* upon the land which the Lord your God is giving you (Exodus 20:12, NKJV, emphasis mine).

The news tells us that child and teenage suicide is at an all-time high. It is easy to connect the spirit of rebellion and the dishonoring of parents to this, whether they are the victims of bullying or not. By teaching our children to honor their parents, we are protecting them. Open communication between the generations is an added help to them. It makes them less alone.

By teaching our children to honor their parents, we are protecting them.

Also give thought to this: If you do not teach your children to respect and honor their mother and father, they can see on earth, how will they know how to respect and honor their Heavenly Father that they cannot see? You are their filter.

Ungrateful

> For even though they knew God [as the Creator], they did not honor Him as God or give thanks [for His wondrous creation]. On the contrary, they became worthless in their thinking [godless, with pointless reasonings, and silly speculations], and their foolish heart was darkened. (Romans 1:21 AMP)

We are supposed to come into God's house with praise and thanksgiving. That's how we enter his gates. Gates represent influence and authority. Since God is our authority, he should be our influence. The way outlined in the Bible to approach him is with thanksgiving. The Enemy wants us to be ungrateful. If we are ungrateful, the things we are trying to do will be futile. This verse says their thinking became worthless. I don't know about you, but I don't want to be worthless. I want to be valuable to our Heavenly Father and his kingdom and I want to make my family valuable too. The worst thing we can be is ungrateful to God. I don't know your circumstances, but I've had some hard battles in seasons of my life and immense warfare, and you probably have experienced the same. If you can sit there and say you have nothing to be thankful for, you need a heart check. There is always something to be thankful for—even if the only good thing you can see right now is that you woke up today. Jesus died for you, and you can be thankful for that. In fact, our lives should be something that we give thanks for. Every morning we take a breath is a gift, and that should be the greatest source of our thanks. Let's not overlook it.

> When I consider Your heavens, the work of Your fingers, the moon and the stars, which You have ordained, what is man that You are mindful of him, and the son of man that You visit him? For You have made him a little lower than the angels, and You have crowned him with glory and honor. (Psalm 8:3-5 NKJV)

> Lord, make me to know my end, and what is the measure of my days, that I may know how frail I am. Indeed, You have made my days as handbreadths, and my age is as nothing before You; certainly every man at his best state is but vapor. (Psalm 39:4-5 NKJV)

We need to be thankful for the little things and the big things, the profound miracles, as well as the miracle of life. When we truly think about ourselves with a sober mindset, what is a man that the Lord of Heaven is mindful of him or her, especially when at our best state we are but vapor? Our days are very short, so we should be thankful for every breath the Lord grants us.

Unloving

> They will be unloving and unforgiving; they will slander others and have no self-control. They will be cruel and hate what is good. (2 Timothy 3:3 NLT)

> But I say to you, love your enemies, bless those who curse you, do good to those who hate you, and pray for those who spitefully use you and persecute you. (Matthew 5:44 NKJV)

> There is no fear in love; but perfect love casts out fear, because fear involves torment. But he who fears has not been made perfect in love. We love Him because He first loved us. If someone says, "I love God," and hates his brother, he is a liar; for he who does not love his brother whom he has seen, how can he love God whom he has not seen? And this commandment we have from Him: that he who loves God must love his brother also. (1 John 4:18-21 NKJV)

Our faith in Christ should lead us to love all people everywhere. All of us are God's children. We can say we love them all we want, but if we are truly showing love, there will be fruit. In these verses, God shows us that loving him and loving his children go hand in hand. They are connected.

In 1 Corinthians 13, Paul gives us the definition of what love is. While reading this, you should replace your name where the word *love* appears. If you cannot say any part of it like that, then that is an area you need to grow in, and that's okay. That's what the Word is supposed to do—help us see our heart's condition. The Word of God is alive and active and sharper than any double-edged sword. Allow the Word to convict you and transform you. By doing so, you will close off any doorways where weeds may grow unhindered. Don't allow an unloving heart to be a foothold for the Enemy.

> Love is patient and kind. Love is not jealous or boastful or proud or rude. It does not demand its own way. It is not irritable, and it keeps no record of being wronged. It does not rejoice about injustice but rejoices whenever the truth wins out. Love never gives up, never loses faith, is always hopeful, and endures through every circumstance. (1 Corinthians 13:4-7 NLT)

Note how love's attributes are the exact opposite of the verses we looked at in 2 Timothy. Love's attributes keep the foxes from creeping into the vineyard of our hearts because God is love. He is all those things, so naturally, abiding in him and who he is, will keep all the other things at bay.

> And above all things have fervent love for one another, for "love will cover a multitude of sins." (1 Peter 4:8 NKJV)

It's not just the people in the pews that are covered by God's love, but *all* people everywhere.

It's not just your sin, my friend, that love covers, but the sin of *all* of us. It's not just the people in the pews that are covered by God's love, but *all* people everywhere. However, we have become unloving and unkind to one another. We quickly tend to point our fingers, as if we are above sin. Yet we all sin! Thank the Lord that his love covers sin. I'm not saying we are all going to be best friends, holding hands, and singing *kumbaya*, but real love, peppered with grace and seasoned with compassion, goes a long way, and can make a big difference. If we aren't showing love, we need to examine our heart in a big way. Jesus literally told us to love even our enemies. God told us that if we don't love people, we can't possibly love him. Yes, some are harder to love than others, but we need to grow in love to really reflect God to the world around us.

Unforgiving

"And whenever you stand praying, if you have anything against anyone, forgive him, that your Father in heaven may also forgive you your trespasses. But if you do not forgive, neither will your Father in heaven forgive your trespasses." (Mark 11:25-26 NKJV)

Let's be honest. We, as a people, are the worst grudge-holders ever. Some of us have things against others and don't even know why. Unforgiveness can be passed down from generation to generation. Too often we pass down hate and unforgiveness instead of letting it go. We teach our kids that "we don't talk to those people."

However, the Bible literally tells us that if we don't forgive, He doesn't forgive us. If unforgiveness goes unchecked, it takes root and turns into pride and bitterness. And pride and bitterness are the root causes of pretty much every evil stronghold and spirit that exists. The war is real. The time has come. Let. It. Go.

Think about this: Most all of us that have been raised in church have the Lord's Prayer memorized and have said it thousands of times over the course of our lives. Even if you are new to the faith and don't have it memorized, the odds are that you are familiar with its contents. You may have heard it in a movie or been around people who've recited it. The words *debtors* and *trespassers* may have been swapped out according to which church you attended, but they mean essentially the same thing—someone who has wronged you or sinned against you. Jesus prayed like this:

> In this manner, therefore, pray: Our Father in heaven, hallowed be Your name. Your kingdom come. Your will be done on earth as it is in heaven. Give us this day our daily bread. *And forgive us our debts, as we forgive our debtors.* And do not lead us into temptation, but deliver us from the evil one. For Yours is the kingdom and the power and the glory forever. Amen. (Matthew 6:9-13 NKJV, emphasis mine)

Do you understand these words that many mindlessly pray? This is a request to God for him to forgive you as you forgive others! If you have a list of wrongs that you constantly rehearse and a string of people you won't talk to because of a grudge, this is a scary thought. Do you want to be forgiven by God? Then you need to be forgiving others. If a pure and holy God who has not sinned can forgive them, who are you (a sinner like them) to sit in judgment and not forgive them? Allow the Holy Spirit to do a work in you and reveal any unforgiveness in your heart, so you can repent.

Slanderers

> The wise of heart will receive commands, but a babbling fool will come to ruin. (Proverbs 10:8 NASB)

> Whoever secretly slanders his neighbor, him I will destroy; I will not endure one who has a haughty look and an arrogant heart. (Psalm 101:5 NASB)

I love how many proverbs and other scriptures are about the tongue. God literally put-up warning signs like, "Hello! Are you listening? Zip thy lip!" Allowing our tongues to be foolish and flap and cluck, not only gets us into trouble, but brings retribution; it says they will be destroyed. The psalm points out how those things spoken in secret come to the light in the end. We tend to think that if it's in private, it's okay, and it's not hurting anyone, but slander is slander. The Bible says that out of the abundance of the heart, the mouth speaks. Are you speaking slander? If so, slander is in your heart.

> No weapon formed against you shall prosper, *and every tongue which rises against you in judgment you shall condemn.* This is the heritage of the servants of the Lord, and their righteousness is from Me," says the Lord. (Isaiah 54:17 NKJV, emphasis mine)

This verse is often wielded in warfare prayer. It is a declaration that nothing the Enemy throws at you will prosper, but the second half of it is the promise of the condemnation of the tongues that have risen against us. If you slander another, you could be the reason someone is experiencing warfare. They may or may not know it was you that started it, but the Lord knows. And your tongue will be condemned. We are told as children that if you don't have anything nice to say, *don't say anything at all*. This is a biblical principle too.

By using our tongue for slander and hate, we give the Enemy legal access

> Don't use foul or abusive language. Let everything you say be good and helpful, so that your words will be an encouragement to those who hear them. (Ephesians 4:29 NLT)

By using our tongue for slander and hate, we give the Enemy legal access into our lives. Additionally, we come under the wrath of the Almighty. He will protect his children.

Self-control

For the Spirit God gave us does not make us timid, but gives us power, love and self-discipline. (2 Timothy 1:7 NIV)

Like a city that is broken into and without walls so is a person who has no self-control over his spirit. (Proverbs 25:28 NASB)

A person with self-control has balance in their life. However, we often see the reverse: people who have lost control of their tongues, attitudes, food, temper, and more. That's all before we even factor in addictions and other self-destructive practices. If we are lacking self-control, we are on a road to destruction. If we do not have self-control, we will live as slaves to those things which we cannot master.

Brutality

According to *Strong's Exhaustive Concordance*, the word *brutal* means "fierce, savage, and not tame"[10] and it only appears here in 2 Timothy 3:3. Today's culture glorifies brutality, but it's not something we should seek after. Have you ever witnessed a horrible fight, and thought, *"That was brutal!"* The word *savage* is also used as a racial slur towards Native Americans and any people group considered uncivilized. In the movie *Pocahontas*, this term was used. The Europeans called the native population of Virginia savages. They considered them barely human, as though they were worse than wild animals. It was an insult. This same evil way of regarding others is creeping into our culture again and spreading. We need to wake up and recognize this evil and stop it.

"Behold, I send you out as sheep in the midst of wolves. Therefore be wise as serpents and harmless as doves." (Matthew 10:16 NKJV)

---

10. James Strong, "434. Anémeros," *Strong's Exhaustive Concordance*: Greek 434. ἀνήμερος (Anémeros) -- not tame, accessed May 31, 2022, https://biblehub.com/strongs/greek/434.htm.

Through patience a ruler may be persuaded, and a gentle
tongue breaks bone. (Proverbs 25:15 NASB)

Kindness and gentleness are not the same as weakness, and we do
not have to be brutal to be strong. Greater strength flows from a gentle
heart, and it will beat out fierce brutality every time. It's called meek-
ness and if you need an example of it, look at the cross.

Despisers of Good

We see this now more than ever before. This world despises God so
much that you are allowed to speak about every other kind of god on
TV and in speeches, but not the one true God. Think about this honestly.
The language on your TV includes references to every kind of lady part,
man part, and all kinds of foul speech imaginable, but showing a Bible,
a cross, or a Christian is frowned upon. We have allowed the courts to
remove God from our schools, and those institutions need him more
than ever. Worldwide, Christians are mocked and beheaded for believing in God. Right here in the United States, loving God has become
synonymous with being a racist hypocrite! Who's selfish? A real whiney
Karen anti-vaxxer, that's who. It may sound funny, but it's the truth.
Why? It's the fruit of despising God. God is the ultimate good—everything good about us is because of him and from him. In Isaiah 5:20, it
says woe to you who call evil good, and good evil! That is exactly what
we are seeing culturally today!

Traitors, headstrong, haughty, lovers of pleasure rather
than lovers of God. (2 Timothy 3:4 NKJV)

Paul really preached and spoke the truth. He wasn't afraid to deliver
hard words when needed. We should desire more of Paul's messages.
We don't need our flesh fluffed. We don't need to listen to rainbow and
unicorn messages. We need to hear the real gospel, the truth speakers,
who will tell us that if we don't stop playing with fire, we *will* end up
getting burned. We have played with the Enemy's fire for far too long.

It's time to cut it out and give way to God's refining fire in our hearts. Our goal should be to live for him with our eyes on heaven, and we should take others with us. Let the truth stand up. If your pastor does not take a hard stance on sin, you may want to find a new pastor. A good pastor wants you to live a consecrated life and make heaven your home.

2 Timothy 3:5 says there are those who are "holding to the form of godliness but denying its power," and that we "should avoid these people." Dr. Tony Evans says this verse means "to project a religious appearance absent of true spiritual reality." Religion without the presence and power of God is like wax fruit: It looks real, but it's fake and possesses no nutritional value. True godliness moves people from sin to righteousness.

Religion without the presence and power of God is like wax fruit.

Lord, help us! We do not want to be those who appear to have you when we don't. This is such a sobering verse. We love to dress things up and paint a picture of how great everything will be. We can put lipstick on a pig, but it's still going to be a pig. We can easily justify sin and make it okay in our minds, but in reality, it is not.

> For whoever shall keep the whole law, and yet stumble in one point, he is guilty of all. For He who said, "Do not commit adultery," also said, "Do not murder." Now if you do not commit adultery, but you do murder, you have become a transgressor of the law. (James 2:10-11 NKJV)

We must not fall into this religious trap. We might maintain a godly form by not stealing or being an alcoholic, but if you are gossiping, you are no better than the one who does those other things. In truth, the One who commands us not to get drunk in Proverbs 23:20 is the same One who also commands us not to gossip in Ephesians 4:29.

Those who consider themselves religious and yet do not keep a tight rein on their tongues deceive themselves, and their religion is worthless. (James 1:26 NIV)

We don't want to play church, dressing up and acting a part. We need to be the real thing—people that move others from sin to our Father, and who walk in his power and his call, allowing him to purify and refine us. We can only pretend for so long. The façade will fall apart; it always does. Get this in your heart. You don't have to fake it until you make it! You might be able to fool everyone around you, but you could never fool God. Submit to his process and change day by day, step-by-step. Who would choose to be a striving and unhappy counterfeit when they could be authentic and joyful instead?

You don't have to fake it until you make it!

For of this sort are those who creep into households and make captives of gullible women loaded down with sins, led away by various lusts. (2 Timothy 3:6 NKJV)

Let's break this down a little. It's a clear warning to us. The word translated "creep" is the Greek *enduno* and means "I clothe, I enter, creep into, to envelop in, to hide in, to put on, insinuate oneself into."[11] All these evils come stealthily and slowly until you are fully clothed (or enveloped) in all these terrible things.

Sin literally wants to be worn like clothing. It wants to enter your dwelling, and have you plant it in your garden, so it can choke out everything around it. It makes captives of gullible women. A primary example is the first woman, Eve. The serpent crept in with his lies and took her mind captive. This caused the fall of mankind.

11. James Strong, "1744. Endunó," Strong's Greek: 1744. ἐνδύνω (endunó) -- creep., accessed May 31, 2022, https://biblehub.com/greek/1744.htm.

Men, let me tell you something. This verse may reference women, but sin will do the same to you. If not, Adam wouldn't have fallen for the same trap.

The word for "captive" is aichmalōtizō and means "to take or lead captive, to subdue or ensnare."[12] The NASB translation renders this "making a prisoner." If we dig a little deeper, we find that it means "to subjugate, bring under control, to take captive one's mind, and lead away captive."

It may seem harmless at first, but it bears terrible fruit. We are easily distracted by our surroundings and other interests. Missing church to entertain yourself by going to a concert occasionally is fine, but when it becomes habitual, our church commitment recedes into the background of our life at a rapid rate. Missing your time with God once in while isn't the end of the world, but when that time falls away completely, we're on a slippery slope. The more we separate ourselves from pursuing God with our time, the more we fill life with our own desires. Slowly, we can lose our step with Jesus, and wander.

We tell ourselves we are only committing a small sin. There is no such thing as a small sin, my friend. Sin is sin. Even one carries the death sentence. Sin wants to creep into your home and put you in bondage. Remember, it's the *little* foxes that spoil the vine. What seems like a small thing, when allowed to grow unchecked, will cause you to be twisted and tangled up before you even realize you are in trouble. That's why it's important to recognize this process. Don't get me wrong. We all fall short, walk into a trap, or do wrong, but when we recognize it, and repent, God will help us change.

2 Timothy 3:7 also describes those who are "always learning and never able to come to a knowledge of the truth." Surprisingly, we can always be learning, but not coming to the knowledge of truth! Let's look at another verse. 1 Timothy 2:4 says that God "wants everyone to be saved and to come to the knowledge of the truth."

---

12. James Strong, "G163 - Aichmalōtizō - Strong's Greek Lexicon (KJV)," Blue Letter Bible, accessed May 31, 2022, https://www.blueletterbible.org/lexicon/g163/kjv/tr/0-1/.

In this verse "knowledge" is the Greek *epignósis,* which means "recognition or knowledge" and specifically the "knowledge of a particular point (directed towards a particular object) perception, discernment, recognition, intuition."[13] It connects to *gnosis* which refers to "knowledge gained through firsthand relationship."[14]

Everything always goes back to relationship. You can read the Bible until you know every hidden gem, but if you're not applying it and having a relationship with God, letting him transform you, then you are just reading and you are not coming to the knowledge of the truth. We must have a relationship and apply what we learn. Regular knowledge comes from reading books and education. We call that "book smarts." However, the true knowledge of God comes from relationship with the Father. I encourage you today to kick out the things that are creeping into you, your house, and your family. Start looking to Jesus, the Author and Finisher of our faith. Focus on forging a great relationship with him.

We must have a relationship and apply what we learn.

Start today by reading 1 Timothy 4:12-16. The choice is yours.

Life is full of choices and decisions. We make them every single day, and every one of them has a consequence. Newton's Third Law of Motion says that "for every action, there is an equal and opposite reaction." Some of those consequences are visible in the natural, but some are in our spirit and affect our walk with the Lord. They affect the spirit man.

Poor spiritual consequences are not fun. They include choosing to hold a grudge. We must choose to fight or walk away, gossip or pray, engage an enemy or turn the other cheek. We can't control what others do or what others say, but we can control our actions and responses. I

---

13. James Strong, "1922. Epignósis," Strong's Greek: 1922. ἐπίγνωσις (epignósis) -- recognition, knowledge, accessed May 31, 2022, https://biblehub.com/greek/1922.htm.

14. James Strong, "1108. Gnosis," Strong's Greek: 1108. γνῶσις (GNÓSIS) -- a knowing, knowledge, accessed May 31, 2022, https://biblehub.com/greek/1108.htm.

can't control how others treat me, but I can control how I treat them. Our actions and reactions are up to us; we get to make those choices, and we will have to live with the consequence of what we have sown.

We have the power to not react.

We cannot blame other people for our knee-jerk reactions and poor choices; we must own our decisions, good or bad. People say things like this:

"I only said that because you said that to me."

"If you didn't want me to say something, you should not have done that to me."

We have a million justifications as to why we blame another instead of accepting responsibility. We've all done this, but blame is a deadly disease. We need to understand that we have the power to not react. It's our choice, not theirs. By blaming the other person, we are unknowingly giving them power over us. We become slaves to their actions. We must have the strength to realize that we have the gift to choose. We have the gift to submit our trouble to God and respond according to his unction. We have a choice. Let's define that.

According to *Merriam-Webster Online*, a "choice" is defined as:

1: the act of choosing: selection, as in finding it hard to make a *choice*

2: power of choosing: option: You have no *choice*

3a: the best part: cream: Of the cavalry, the king's own was the *choice*.

b: a person or thing chosen: She was their first *choice*

4: a number and variety to choose among: A plan with a wide *choice* of options

5: care in selecting

6: a grade of meat between prime and good: to be preferred

9

David's Choices

Let's examine this further. David is a good example of choices. While he made many good ones, he also made lots of bad ones too.

Now Saul and they and all the men of Israel were in the Valley of Elah, fighting with the Philistines. So David rose early in the morning, left the sheep with a keeper, and took the things and went as Jesse had commanded him. And he came to the camp as the army was going out to the fight and shouting for the battle. For Israel and the Philistines had drawn up in battle array, army against army. And David left his supplies in the hand of the supply keeper, ran to the army, and came and greeted his brothers. Then as he talked with them, there was the champion, the Philistine of Gath, Goliath by name, coming up from the armies of the Philistines; and he spoke according to the same words. *So David heard them.* And all the men of Israel, when they saw the man, fled from him and were dreadfully afraid. So the men of Israel said, "Have you seen this man who has come up? Surely he has come up to defy Israel; and it shall be that the man who kills him the king will enrich with great riches, will give him his daughter, and give his father's house exemption from taxes in Israel." Then David spoke to the men who stood by him, saying, "What shall be done for the man who kills this Philistine and takes away the reproach from Israel? For who is this uncircumcised Philistine, that he should defy the armies of the living God?" (1 Samuel 17:19-26 NKJV, emphasis mine)

You cannot help but notice David's question. Who is this guy that he should defy the armies of the living God? He is asking the right question and looking at the problem the right way.

Then David said to Saul, "Let no man's heart fail because of him; your servant will go and fight with this Philistine." And Saul said to David, "You are not able to go against this Philistine to fight with him; for you are a youth, and he a man of war from his youth." (1 Samuel 17:32-33 NKJV)

If someone is pointing you to a choice that doesn't line up with God's Word, you would be wise not to listen.

As soon as you make a right decision, something or someone will show up to make you doubt it or suggest that it's the wrong choice. Sometimes the person making you feel this way doesn't even know they are being used like that. They have no idea that their advice is diverting you from a correct spiritual decision and urging you to a worldly one instead. Often, they sound wise, but it's important to follow the Holy Spirit. He will guide you in all truth and point you the right way. If someone is pointing you to a choice that doesn't line up with God's Word, you would be wise not to listen. When you know you are doing what God directed, don't let anyone come in and fill you with a spirit of doubt. God is not the author of confusion. The Enemy is the author of confusion. When God wants you to do something, he will make it clear.

Some may offer a "godly perspective," giving us "godly advice" with good intentions, but if part of that advice isn't encouraging you to pray and be led by the Spirit, make sure you test the spirit ministering to you.

> Your servant has killed both lion and bear; and this uncircumcised Philistine will be like one of them, seeing he has defied the armies of the living God." Moreover David said, *"The Lord, who delivered me from the paw of the lion and from the paw of the bear, He will deliver me from the hand of this Philistine."* And Saul said to David, "Go, and the Lord be with you!" (1 Samuel 17:36-37 NKJV, emphasis mine)

I love what David is showing us here. It's important to remember who God is and what he's done for us. When we remember what God has already brought us through, all the victories we have walked in, the miracles we have witnessed, and the wars he has helped us win, it helps ignite the warrior within, enabling us to stand firm, knowing that he will help us and do it again. Yes, yes, he will.

He is a do-it-again God. He is not a one and done kind of Lord. Look at everything he has brought you and your family through. Let it fuel the fire of your faith to help you stand in the next battle. Has he ever left you? Why would Christ bring you to this point just to leave you? He wouldn't! Let all you have achieved with him give you the courage to face the next step with him. He does not call us onto the water to let us drown. Remember Peter.

Often our private battles and private victories are the things that strengthen us for the public battles and public victories. It was only David, the stars in the sky, and the eyes of God who witnessed David's private battles and victories in the field with his sheep. David had been forged for this moment through those earlier experiences. He knew that. He understood that God was always at his side—no matter what. The Enemy's appearance was not daunting to David. Whether he looked like a lion, or a giant made no difference. Just because the skin of his enemy had changed did not mean that God had changed. Victory is always our portion, but we must decide to make the choice and walk in it.

> Then David said to the Philistine, *"You come to me with a sword, with a spear,* and with a javelin. *But I come to you in the name of the Lord of hosts,* the God of the armies of Israel, whom you have defied. This day the Lord will deliver you into my hand, and *I will strike you and take your head from you.* And this day I will give the carcasses of the camp of the Philistines to the birds of the air and the wild beasts of the earth, that all the earth may know that there is a God in Israel. *Then all this assembly shall know that the Lord does not save with sword and spear; for the battle is the Lord's, and He will give you into our hands."* (1 Samuel 17:45-47 NKJV, emphases mine)

When we follow God, it's important to let *him* lead the battles. We are not meant to run out and wage war every time something or someone challenges us. In fact, nine times out of ten, challenges are fleshly situations from which we should flee instead of engaging. God must be in control. If we run out to wage spiritual warfare without God, we will be slaughtered in two seconds flat—just like the sons of Sceva. The battle belongs to God. He is the General and we are the soldiers. A general gives the orders and strategies, and good soldiers go out and perform them. If they have been trained well, they may even be in an elite unit with special tasks to perform, but no soldier (elite or otherwise) does anything without orders. Neither do they get sent out unequipped or unprepared. We really need to learn to let God lead. We only need to follow his command.

Here we also see a key principle. David chose to walk in victory. Are you choosing to be the victim or the victor? Are you telling your giants how damaged you are? Or are you telling your giants the condition they are going to be in once God gets through with them? David tells Goliath that he's going to strike him and remove his head. He prophesied his own victory and spoke life into the situation. We must remember the power of our words and choose them wisely.

> So David *prevailed* over the Philistine with a sling and a stone, *and struck the Philistine and killed him. But there was no sword* in the hand of David." (1 Samuel 17:50 NKJV, emphases mine)

David prophesied this victory, and it happened exactly how he said it was going to happen. Imagine how the situation might have turned out if he had trembled and chose to speak negatively. This is a key battle strategy. David was led by the Spirit to act, and he was led by the Spirit to prophesy his victory. When you are flowing in the Holy Spirit, there's no way you can get tripped up in battle.

David didn't need fancy weapons or extensive training because he was listening to the Lord. We tend to think that if we have the most expensive weapons or the best armor money can buy, then we are ready, and we can win. However, decisions based on how we value our weapons and armor are never good ones. We cannot choose our weapons with our fleshly eyes. Our battles are not carnal, so we cannot use real swords, guns, or fists. Just as an atheist regards the Bible as a dusty old book and a useless weapon, so did Goliath consider David's sling and his rocks as of no account and useless. Both the Philistine and the atheist fail to see the weapons for what they really are: deadly. The power did not reside in the sling or stone itself, but in the power of God behind it. It's the same thing with our Bibles. The Word of God is alive and active and sharper than any double-edged sword, and the proper way to wield it is to choose to step aside and let Jesus take the lead.

The Bible is full of stories in which God championed an underdog. Throughout history, God used the most unusual weapons to do extraordinary things through his people. Shamgar used an ox goad to strike down 600 Philistines. (Judges 3:31) Jael, a woman, used a mallet and a tent peg to kill Sisera in her tent. (Judges 4:21) Gideon and his army of only 300 used jars, torches, and trumpets. (Judges 7) An unnamed wise woman used a millstone to crush Abimelech's head. (Judges 9) Samson used the jawbone of a donkey to kill a thousand men. (Judges 15)

It's not about the weapons or the people involved. It is about the Lord. If he tells you to go forth, you can never go wrong. Just follow his commands and instructions. He will do the rest. Just make the choice to listen.

David made many good choices in his life and did mighty and great things for God. He wrote beautiful psalms. Entwined with his stories and those of his mighty men and their victories, we see his wise decisions and his obedience, but we also see something else. He sinned a lot and followed those poor decisions with true repentance. We can easily trace the evils that crept in and the works of the flesh that led him astray. Afterward, we see him truly reflecting and changing. We can learn from his bad choices as well as his good ones, but sadly, we sometimes learn more from the bad. Like David, we get ourselves in quagmires in which we cannot find a way out. Like David, we call on God for help, for a supernatural GPS. David shows us that he was just as human and prone to error as we are.

> Then it happened one evening that David arose from his bed and walked on the roof of the king's house. And from the roof he saw a woman bathing, and the woman was very beautiful to behold. So David sent and inquired about the woman. And someone said, "Is this not Bathsheba, the daughter of Eliam, the wife of Uriah the Hittite?" Then David sent messengers, and took her; and she came to him, and he lay with her, for she was cleansed from her impurity; and she returned to her house. And the woman conceived; so she sent and told David, and said, "I am with child." (2 Samuel 11:2-5 NKJV)

For all that is secret will eventually be brought into the open, and everything that is concealed will be brought to light and made known to all. (Luke 8:17 NLT)

By choosing to sin, you are sowing a seed into something that you do not want to reap.

Just because you can hide a sin from people does not mean you can hide it from God. By choosing to sin, you are sowing a seed into something that you do not want to reap. Jesus taught this, warning us that nothing is truly secret. It will get out. And when it gets out, it will cause humiliation, pain, and shame. That is a battle you can avoid altogether by letting God take the lead in every choice you make and living a life of integrity *all the time:* even behind closed doors. Living a life fully surrendered to God and letting him into every area of your life protects us from reaping the results of hidden sin.

And David said to Uriah, "Go down to your house and wash your feet." So Uriah departed from the king's house, and a gift of food from the king followed him. But Uriah slept at the door of the king's house with all the servants of his lord, and did not go down to his house. (2 Samuel 11:8-9)KJV)

In the morning it happened that David wrote a letter to Joab and sent it by the hand of Uriah. And he wrote in the letter, saying, "Set Uriah in the forefront of the hottest battle, and retreat from him, that he may be struck down and die." (2 Samuel 11:14-15 NKJV)

To cover up one sin, you often must commit another. Before you know it, you are buried under the weight of your deadly decisions, the flesh is striving, and the spirit is being quenched. This is such a sad truth and explains why it is so easy for us to give way to the flesh, but so hard to truly submit to God.

David was desperately trying to cover his tracks. First, he tried to trick Uriah into going home and sleeping with his wife, so he would think the baby was his. This was manipulation, a form of witchcraft David tried to use. But Uriah was an honorable man. It did not work. This poor man was loyal to David and to Israel, but David ordered that he be sent to the front of the battle and left alone so he would be killed. David did not want his sin to be exposed.

Was David unknowingly being used in that moment as a tool for the Enemy? It seems like it. In David's right state of mind, he would never have sacrificed someone so loyal and good. He had Uriah killed in cold blood! But David was being led by his flesh, and in so doing, he was used to destroy someone valuable to the kingdom of Israel.

We must be careful not to provide a foothold for the Enemy when we choose to do wrong and make sinful decisions. Just like David, he could also use us to harm our brothers and sisters in Christ, people who are valuable to the kingdom of heaven. Here's the thing about choices. We often think we are the only ones affected by them, but in fact, when we make a choice, it is like dropping a stone in a lake. The rock hits the surface and sinks to the ground, but the ripples cause the waves to crash against the shore, startling the frogs and sending them back to the safety in the weeds. Under the surface, those the effects still travel, disturbing fish and causing them to dart away from the sudden movement. Our choices have a ripple effect that disturbs, and sometimes even startles, those around us.

Don't we do this though? Can we be honest with ourselves today? We do something wrong, instead of making it right and saying we did it, don't we sometimes make matters worse by trying to hide and cover our sin? Then, like David, we end up in an even worse situation because in covering our tracks, we commit more sin and make more bad decisions. How much easier would it have been to just stop in the beginning, and do the right thing? Our flesh tries to tell us not to tell the truth, to sweep it under the rug, but if you take dirt and keep sweeping it under a rug, it will eventually be noticeable. All that effort trying to hide it and cover it up will be in vain in the end.

> When the wife of Uriah heard that Uriah her husband was dead, she mourned for her husband. And when her mourning was over, David sent and brought her to his house, and she became his wife and bore him a son. *But the thing that David had done displeased the Lord.* (2 Samuel 11:26-27 NKJV, emphasis mine)

How sad! David displeased the Lord. That word "displeased" translates from the Hebrew and means "to be evil, bad."[15] David did evil in the Lord's sight. Imagine that. After doing so many great things for the Lord, David displeased God. We do this too, but we don't like to admit it. When I read this, I can't help but think of Genesis 6 when God regretted making mankind and was grieved in his heart. I do not ever want to grieve the Lord or do evil in his sight. We are all human and will fail sometimes and make bad choices, but what we do after that is equally as important.

There is a way that seems right to a man, but its end is the way of death.

> "Why have you despised the commandment of the Lord, to do evil in His sight? You have killed Uriah the Hittite with the sword; you have taken his wife to be your wife, and have killed him with the sword of the people of Ammon. Now therefore, the sword shall never depart from your house, because you have despised Me, and have taken the wife of Uriah the Hittite to be your wife.' Thus says the Lord: 'Behold, I will raise up adversity against you from your own house; and I will take your

---

15. James Strong, "7489. Ra'a'," Strong's Hebrew: 7489. עָרַ (ra'a') -- afflict, accessed May 31, 2022, https://biblehub.com/hebrew/7489.htm.

wives before your eyes and give them to your neighbor, and he shall lie with your wives in the sight of this sun. *For you did it secretly, but I will do this thing before all Israel, before the sun.'* " So David said to Nathan, *"I have sinned against the Lord."* And Nathan said to David, *"The Lord also has put away your sin; you shall not die.* However, because by this deed you have given great occasion to the enemies of the Lord to blaspheme, *the child also who is born to you shall surely die."* Then Nathan departed to his house. And the Lord struck the child that Uriah's wife bore to David, and it became ill. (2 Samuel 12:9-15 NKJV, emphases mine)

This is what we so often forget. Yes, we are forgiven, but we still need to come face-to-face with the consequences of our sinful behavior. David's sin was forgiven. The Lord had forgiven him, but David reaped the consequences of his forgiven sin just the same. Just because we live under grace does not make us immune to this. We are saved, so we will not die; but in the end, we will reap what we have sown. Even with forgiveness, we must still face the consequence of our poor choices.

Then on the seventh day it came to pass that the child died. And the servants of David were afraid to tell him that the child was dead. For they said, "Indeed, while the child was alive, we spoke to him, and he would not heed our voice. How can we tell him that the child is dead? He may do some harm!" (2 Samuel 12:18 KJV)

David paid the ultimate price; it makes me sad just to think about it. He lost his baby. Every single one of our choices has a consequence, for good or ill. I don't want to see any of us suffer the consequences of bad choices. I want to see us learn to make good choices and reap their rewards. We can do better, and we must do better. If we don't, how can we teach future generations to do the same?

We can't give them what we don't have. We aren't promised lives full of rainbows and sunshine all the time. But when we follow God, we make better choices, and when we stick with him, it's an easier load to carry. When we walk with Christ, we know he is with us in the storm, in the battle, in the hard times. We know he is an ever-present help in our times of need. Let Jesus lead you and make the choices he would have you make. You have free will, so the choice is yours he will not force you, but he will guide you if you let him. Let's review these verses:

> In all your ways acknowledge Him, and He shall direct your paths. (Proverbs 3:6 NKJV)

> So you may walk in the way of goodness, and keep to the paths of righteousness. (Proverbs 2:20 NKJV)

> Ponder the path of your feet, and let all your ways be established. (Proverbs 4:26 NKJV)

Always take the time to stop and think, pray, read your Word, fast, and ask God for wisdom and discernment before you make decisions. Don't make hasty ones; instead, be patient. Wait on the Lord. Follow the leading of the Holy Spirit. Because we reap what we sow, we bring a lot of hard times on ourselves whenever we choose to sow in the flesh. This is a universal truth, affecting everyone on the planet, whether they are aware of it or not. Making wrong choices is your call. Just because someone is giving you negative seed or angry seed, or the seed of discord, bitterness, or jealousy, does not mean you have to plant and harvest it.

You don't have to grow every seed that flies your way. We are human, so we will stumble and fall. When you do, choose not to listen to the condemnation of the Enemy. Follow the conviction of the Holy Spirit instead. Get up, repent, let it go, and move on. Learn from it and grow. Whatever you do, don't make David's choice to cover it up. It really is a slippery slope.

God loved David, even in his bad choices, and called David a man after his own heart. God is with us in our battles too—even those we caused ourselves. David served and prayed, but most of all, he always repented and humbled his heart before God. However, David made some choices that he didn't have to make. The same is true for us.

10

Time to Take Out the Trash

What's the first thing you think about when you hear the word "garbage"? My mind instantly thinks of a rotting dumpster on a hot city day. It smells terrible, its rotting, decomposing, disgusting contents just reek. Someone's nasty, leaking garbage can turn your stomach in a split second, so we rarely even approach a trash can.

What is worse is that we are doing it in our own spiritual homes as well. Spiritually many of us are not only letting the Enemy dump stinking and rotting garbage in our spiritual home, but we are also letting our friends, family, and acquaintances do the same. Some of us have let so much trash and fleshly garbage into our spiritual homes that we have become like a bad episode of Hoarders buried alive. In the natural we take out the trash every week. We don't let it pile up or leak, but in our spirit, we let it pile up, until it is stinking and rotting and out of control! I once had a neighbor who had seven untrained cats. Her house smelled like old urine and ammonia. One day she needed help, and I had trouble even going in because of the smell. Would people want to enter your spiritual house? Or is the garbage out of control?

Untended trash also attracts unwanted pests. One of them as I'm sure you could guess is flies. Flies are nasty little creatures: Every time they land, they poop and salivate so they can eat. They also lay lots of eggs in their short lifetimes. They can be hard to eliminate, especially if the garbage is still present. So why are we talking about flies? Matthew 12:24 says this: "When the Pharisees heard this, they said, 'This man drives out demons only by Beelzebul, the ruler of the demons.'"

Beelzebub was a name for the Devil. The Pharisees were accusing Jesus of driving out Satan's demons in the name of Satan. (Jesus went on to tell them how and why this could not be true.) However, the name Beelzebub comes from the Old Testament and literally means "the lord of flies" or "flying god."[16] Mentioned in 2 Kings 1:2, this title for Satan stresses that he is the prince over demons ("demonic flies"), which agrees with the scripture that calls him the prince of the power of the air in Ephesians 2:2.

Demons love filth. They thrive in it. In Matthew 8, we see demons begging Jesus to allow them to go into a herd of pigs when he casts them out. The demons cannot roam freely. Demons are spiritual beings and require an earthly vessel in which to inhabit. Demons must reside in something that is living, just as the Devil inhabited the serpent in the garden. The Bible says our bodies are a temple for the Holy Spirit to dwell in. Whatever the Lord creates, the Enemy tries to counterfeit. Satan is not equal to God. He too is a creation, and the creation cannot create, only duplicate, what is already made.

So, the demons chose to inhabit the pigs and killed them all. When we picture pigs, we see dirt and filth. Pigs lay around in the mud and slop and eat just about anything, including their own off spring. So, it is not surprising that out of all the other animals the demons could have asked Jesus to cast them into, they chose the pigs. They did not ask to go into the birds or the fish or even another person. No, they chose the pigs.

> When Jesus arrived on the other side of the lake, in the region of the Gadarenes, two men who were possessed by demons met him. They came out of the tombs and *were so violent that no one could go through that area.* They began screaming at him, "Why are you interfering with us, Son of God? Have you come here to torture us before God's appointed time?" There happened to be a large herd of pigs feeding in the distance. So the demons

---

16. James Strong, "954. Beelzeboul," Strong's Greek: 954. Βεελζεβούλ (Beelzeboul) -- beelzebul, a name of Satan, accessed May 31, 2022, https://biblehub.com/greek/954.htm.

begged, *"If you cast us out, send us into that herd of pigs."* "All right, go!" *Jesus commanded them.* So the demons came out of the men and entered the pigs, and the *whole herd plunged down the steep hillside into the lake and drowned in the water.* The herdsmen fled to the nearby town, *telling everyone what happened to the demon-possessed men.* Then the entire town came out to meet Jesus, *but they begged him to go away and leave them alone.* (Matthew 8:28-34 NLT, emphases mine)

Jesus performed a mighty miracle: He delivered two demon-possessed men, setting them free; but the people in the nearby town were terrified. Instead of rejoicing and wanting to spend more time with Jesus, they begged him to go away. Begged him. To *leave.* This is what happens if we choose to focus on the trash and not on the Lord. This is what happens when we are led by fear instead of God. The text does not say that they chased him out of town, but they begged him to leave in the same way the demons begged to be cast into the pigs. Were they only thinking of the loss of the herd and blamed Jesus for that? Did they not value the restoration of the two men from their own village?

The Enemy does this with the trash and filth in our lives. He uses it as a foothold to slide in and destroy us. His goal is to taint a testimony, diminish a miracle, and drive away the presence of the Lord, just like he did in this situation. He still uses the same tactics, so do not think he would not do the same to you. Our enemy is very real, and we are truly fooling ourselves if we think that he isn't after us.

It began to speak blasphemies against God: to blaspheme his name and his dwelling—those who dwell in heaven. And it was permitted to wage war against the saints and to conquer them. It was also given authority over every tribe, people, language, and nation. (Revelation 13:6-7)

The Devil wars with the saints, so don't think he is just sitting around playing Yahtzee and twiddling his fingers. Revelation may specifically speak of the end times, but the tactics are the same. The Bible calls him our adversary, and an adversary is an opponent. Peter tells us our adversary is like a roaring lion seeking whom he may devour. He is also called the accuser of the brethren in Revelation 12:10. An accuser brings formal charges against a person that are binding to exact a penalty. Satan acts as an adversary, bringing the "(law)suit" of darkness against believers for their eternal damnation."[17]

However, the Enemy is not omnipotent (all-powerful). The Enemy is also not omniscience (all-knowing) or omnipresent (everywhere at the same time). Only our God is all those things! The Enemy has limitations. He needs others to help him do his dirty work. He sends out his little evil spirits to do his bidding. They are like nasty, pesky flies, and they are attracted to your garbage. They like those dirty places and spaces that you haven't cleansed—that we have left sitting in a dirty spiritual funk. They aren't attracted to anything clean, so it's vital that we take out our trash.

The Enemy has limitations.

How would you define spiritual trash and garbage beyond sin in general? It includes negative behaviors and attitudes that are breeding grounds in a believer's life. Think for a minute about the prophet Elijah. He was a man of God; he called fire down from heaven, and tore down idols and false gods, and yet, we see him fleeing from Jezebel. Why? She said she would have his head (an outright lie), but *he believed* it.

Spiritual trash also takes the form of repetitive sin patterns, addictions, pornography exposure, cult material, unforgiveness, and deep scars and wounds as the result of physical and mental abuse. These are just a few, but there are many more. If left undealt with and not completely removed, these problems can lead to fear, rejection, anger, bitterness, and even hatred in our hearts. It's not always the things we

---

17. James Strong, "476. Antidikos," Strong's Greek: 476. ἀντίδικος (antidikos) -- an opponent, adversary, accessed May 31, 2022, https://biblehub.com/greek/476.htm.

expect to take root that do; it's often the thing we brush off and sweep under the rug that begins to fester and spoil over time.

At some point in time, we decided as a people that believers are exempt from the problems and abuses the rest of the world had. We don't talk about mental health; we brush off emotional abuse; we normalize dysfunction. We like to pretend that adultery, suicide, addiction, child abuse, mental abuse, physical abuse, depression, anxiety, and the like don't happen amongst our own. But in doing this, we have created a garbage dump for the Enemy and his underlings. People are not getting help because we don't talk about this stuff, but they can't seek outside help because outsiders don't understand. The stigma in the church for the mentally ill is so bad that it can drive them into worse places. They feel unwanted and rejected and unacceptable. This should not be. Jesus never treated people like this.

You name it, and Jesus died to remove it, and make us free.

And the truth is that we are not exempt from these issues. They are present in the body, and we need to start talking about them and exposing them, so we can get real help. People need to know that these are real problems, and that God can fix them. They need to know they aren't alone, that they aren't the only ones. People are deeply wounded, and we as the church need to step up and open the doors for them. We need to accept and love them where they are at, allowing them space to talk about these things. Jesus was pierced for our transgressions, crushed for our sin; the punishment that brought us peace was laid on him. He was stricken and afflicted, but by his wounds, we are healed. That healing covers a multitude of brokenness. It heals us of our sin. Sin refers to separation from God. Jesus healed what Adam and Eve broke in the garden. He heals our bodies, cures cancers, grows kidneys, makes hearts beat again and mends bones. He also heals every type of broken spirit.

Anxiety. Depression. Insecurity. Eating disorders. Gambling addictions. PTSD. You name it, and Jesus died to remove it, and make us free.

His sacrifice heals that hole in your heart that you feel every night right before you fall asleep. It is the cure for the emptiness that we sadly so often feel. We like to paint the picture that our lives are perfect. There is a big difference between wisely not sharing everything and not being honest. It's time for us to be honest. Jesus paid too high of a price for us to let our brothers and sisters build a landfill of issues, which we do not allow them to address or talk about. They need help. There is no shame in any of this. They need to hear the testimonies of those who have dealt with these issues and prevailed through God, so they can begin to receive help. It's time to start truly taking out the trash. We are humans, not gods. We need to start acting like it. It starts with owning what happens to us, not ignoring it away or normalizing or glamorizing it. We must truly deal with it and let the Lord take care of it.

We tend to get all too comfortable with the familiar spirits in our life, as well as the generational spirits. We even make excuses for them. For example, we say things like, "Well, his grandpa was an alcoholic, and his dad was an alcoholic, so that's why he is an alcoholic." We supply this same thought pattern for every type of issue or problem that exists. You can insert your own issue and fill-in-the-blank. However, this is not what God intends. This is not his will for any of us.

We should not use our family's past to justify our present. We can have freedom from all of that. We can choose to be different than our father, mother, siblings, and grandparents. We all have a moment, when we are young, when we realize how wrong this choice is, but as we get older, that thought gets lost as the innocence of youth fades. I am here to remind you of that moment and encourage you with the hope of the freedom Jesus offers you. You don't have to be enslaved to that life pattern. You can be free. It ran in the family until it ran into Jesus-in-you. If we take a stand and decide to break the cycle, and start cleaning up our lives and homes, similar spirits will leave for a time. However, if the emotional patterns are allowed to remain, those doors can lead them right back and the mess we cleaned up will soon be replaced with another one. You need to have a full transformation by renewing your mind in God's Word. That's where the change happens.

> "When an unclean spirit comes out of a person, it roams through waterless places looking for rest but doesn't find any. Then it says, 'I'll go back to my house that I came from.' Returning, it finds the house vacant, swept, and put in order. Then it goes and brings with it seven other spirits more evil than itself, and they enter and settle down there. As a result, that person's last condition is worse than the first. That's how it will also be with this evil generation." (Matthew 12:43-45)

You cannot clean up your home with self-righteousness and participate in religious activities without dealing with these issues. You will only make yourself worse. You also can't clean spiritual problems up with natural solutions, or you will also end up worse. Spiritual problems need spiritual solutions. We need to submit to the Lord and the Holy Spirit to fill the void. Submission is the key to keeping that area free from the familiar spirits coming back. We must give in to the transforming power and sanctification process to grow into new people. Then our house won't just be clean. It will be remodeled!

Spiritual problems need spiritual solutions.

When we take out the garbage at home, we gather everything we can find, including stuff in the fridge, the closet, and the small garbage cans throughout our house. We don't want any garbage left behind. We also don't want to have to make more trips to the dumpster than is absolutely necessary. We go through the whole house, and bag it all up. We tie it off. If it has a leak, we double bag it. Then we immediately take it out of the house and to the dumpster, so the garbage man can take it away. We don't leave that bagged garbage sitting in the house so it can start to decompose and leak. So why are we doing this spiritually? Often, we start cleaning spiritually and leave it in a corner. Never dealing with the full root issues and behaviors that go along with those issues. We just start a nice pile. We think that if we appear clean on the outside, then we are clean, but eventually that stinky stuff is going to come out and spread.

What have you been adding to the garbage stacks in your life? What have you started to clean up, but never finished? In what area are you not giving full submission? Look deep so you can take out that trash!

This garbage is allowing these dirty flies to plague us. Many years ago, I lived in an apartment. One day I came home, and my dining room was swarming with flies. It was like a horror movie. I bought a poisonous spray for flies, sprayed where they had been, vacuumed them up, cleaned the window, and was all pleased with myself. The next morning, I woke up, walked out of my room, and could literally hear them again in the dining room. It looked just like it had the day before. I repeated the whole process, but this time I sprayed outside on the patio and all the window ledges too. To my surprise, when I returned that afternoon they were back again. I ended up calling the apartment complex office for an exterminator. When the exterminator arrived, he looked at the flies and mentioned their color. I asked why that mattered, and he told me that different flies were attracted to different things. My flies were attracted to dead things. He went outside and found a dead bird in a bush and removed it. Needless to say, my tactics had no chance of success because there was a rotting carcass constantly drawing new flies.

11

Understanding the Devil's Hierarchy

N ot only do we have to clean up properly, but we need to understand that different flies are attracted to different things. In other words, not all evil spirits like the same kind of dirt. They are all attracted to something specific.

> For our struggle is not against flesh and blood
> [contending only with physical opponents], but against
> the rulers, against the powers, against the world forces
> of this [present] darkness, against the spiritual forces
> of wickedness in the heavenly (supernatural) places.
> (Ephesians 6:12 AMP)

Our struggles are not with one another. We often think that they are, and get offended easily, but that's a big mistake. Our fight is with the Enemy and his forces. Sometimes the person you think is hurting you is being influenced by a spirit, so your fight isn't actually against them, but against the spirit manipulating them. In this case, it's important to remember that there's a huge difference between being possessed and being oppressed. They are not the same thing

Principalities are ranked and grouped according to their purpose. The Devil tries to replicate God's authority structure, but again, he is only a counterfeiter. Principalities usually operate in places of power, such as government, courts, and the like. They love personalities. These are the foul generals to the Enemy's foot soldiers. Powers refer to "ability, capacity, control, authority, and delegated influence."[18]

Certain roots attract principalities and powers (the Bible pairs these two together). They include moral impurity, bitterness, and greed. Hebrews 12:15 instructs us to watch diligently "so that no one falls short of the grace of God, lest any root of bitterness spring up to cause trouble, and many become defiled by it" (MEV). Greed is an evil root in those who value the temporary above the eternal. They are consumed with money and material things. An example can be found in Exodus when they made and worshiped the golden calf.

The devil has power, but he's not all-powerful.

As we discussed earlier, the devil has power, but he's not all-powerful. He would like to be all-powerful like God, but he's not. He is limited in his power. He can do supernatural things though. We are impressed with supernatural things, and tend to elevate them, but not all that's supernatural is from God. That is why we aren't supposed to be attracted to supernatural things. Cult leaders sometimes make themselves look supernatural to impress people so they will follow them. That's why it's important to not be led by the supernatural. There is even a Hindu spirit called *kundalini* that is being introduced into Western society through yoga practices that is a counterfeit Holy Spirit. Interestingly, it is pictured as a coiled snake at the base of the spine. We are not supposed to be ignorant about the source of anything in our lives. We want to draw from one Source only: God.

> Now the Lord spoke to Moses and to Aaron, saying, "When Pharaoh shall speak to you, saying, 'show a miracle,' then you shall say to Aaron, 'Take your rod, and

---

18. "Power Definition & Meaning," Merriam-Webster (Merriam-Webster), accessed May 31, 2022, https://www.merriam-webster.com/dictionary/power.

throw it before Pharaoh,' and it shall become a serpent."
So Moses and Aaron went to Pharaoh, and they did
what the Lord had commanded. And Aaron threw down
his rod before Pharaoh and before his servants, and it
became a serpent. Then Pharaoh also called the wise men
and the sorcerers. Then the magicians of Egypt likewise
performed with their secret arts. (Exodus 7:8-11 MEV)

Other translations say that Pharoah's wise men accomplished this
feat through occult practices. What if the story stopped there? Would
we be astounded that they were able to duplicate what God did? Picture
what it must have been like for Moses and Aaron as they stood watching, and these magicians who didn't serve their God, turned a rod into a
snake just like God had! What would you think if you had been there?
Would you have been impressed? The Bible goes on to tell us that Aaron's snake ate all of the others, and Moses went on to challenge every
one of their false gods.

This story illuminates why it's not good to be impressed with supernatural wonders. It would have been easy to be amazed by the sorcerers
without understanding the source of their power. Moses and Aaron stood
firm and were not led astray by this seeming miracle. God won the day.

As these verses clearly show, principalities and powers are often
linked together.

> For I am persuaded that neither death nor life, neither
> angels *nor principalities nor powers*, neither things
> present nor things to come, (Romans 8:38 MEV,
> emphasis mine)

> Far above all *principalities, and power,* and might, and
> dominion, and every name that is named, not only in this
> age but also in that which is to come. (Ephesians 1:21 MEV,
> emphasis mine)

So that now the manifold wisdom of God might be made know by the church to the *principalities and powers* in the heavenly places, (Ephesians 3:10 MEV, emphasis mine)

And having disarmed *authorities and powers*, He made a show of them openly, triumphing over them by the cross. (Colossians 2:15 MEV, emphasis mine)

Who has gone into heaven and is at the right hand of God, with angels and *authorities and powers* being made subject to Him. (1 Peter 3:22 MEV, emphasis mine)

In fact, it's a good idea to read the following passages in their entirety, so that you can see the context of what God is saying about them: Ephesians 1:15-23, Ephesians 3:8-12, and Colossians 2:9-15.

What does all this teach us? Why did I make you read all that? First of all, they show how the principalities and powers are connected to one another and feed off each other. However, they also show us that we do not have to walk in fear of them. You probably noticed the other connection: Jesus. Christ put *all these things under his feet* and under his subjection. He took away their ultimate power. We must not walk in fear but wake up and realize who we are and to whom we belong! We belong to the Most High God who allows us to put these things under our feet because he did it first. The church has been given authority over all principalities and powers. Who is the church? You are the church! Since 1 Peter taught us that these spirits are subject to Christ, it's time we began walking in his power and authority. Let's fight the good fight.

The "rulers of darkness" mentioned in Ephesians 6:12 (MEV) govern the areas that have no light. They thrive in ignorance and deception. Darkness is an absence of truth. Lies accepted as truth. What is truth? What is light? God's Word is truth. It is your sword and your only offensive weapon. God's Word is also light. Psalm 119:106 says the "word is a lamp to my feet and a light to my path" (MEV). Light always expels darkness. Truth always expels lies.

Secrets can be demonic territory. I'm not talking about keeping someone's confidence; that is a different thing. However, when we practice secret sins, we open ourselves to demonic attack. That is the reason why James 5:14-16 gives us instructions about how to deal with this:

> Is anyone among you sick? He should call for the elders of the church, and they are to pray over him, anointing him with oil in the name of the Lord. The prayer of faith will save the sick person, and the Lord will raise him up; if he has committed sins, he will be forgiven. Therefore, confess your sins to one another and pray for one another, so that you may be healed. The prayer of a righteous person is very powerful in its effect. (James 5:14-16)

Confession of faults brings healing. Secret sins are like a sickness to your spiritual man.

I'm not telling you to run out and tell everyone, but you should be able to go to another Christian and tell them what is ailing you and get wise counsel and prayer. The Enemy wants to keep you in bondage, and he can do this through the secret sin you keep to yourself, hidden away so you are not getting free. He thrives in ignorance and deception. He thrives in lies; dry and dirty places are his breeding ground.

Confession of faults brings healing.

Our battleground begins in our mind. If the Devil can keep you in the wrong mindset, he can hold you captive. We are supposed to take captive every thought, to make it obedient to Christ. The Enemy wants us to focus on the wrong things, so we can't focus on the right ones. He loves to paint pictures, so our fleshly imaginations can run wild. We are to cast down these imaginations. However, the Devil is sly and cunning; he uses our gateways to fool us. He likes to orchestrate things, so he distorts what we see.

Jesus is the Light of the World, and light always expels darkness. If you walk into a dark room, and switch on a light, the darkness disappears. It can be completely pitch black, but once you get to a lamp and turn it on, it's no longer dark. That is how God is too. His truth is light, and his light dispels darkness (the Enemy's lies and much, much more). If you are being defeated, it could be because you don't know your Word. If you don't know your Word, you don't know what the truth is. Knowing the truth will help you identify the lies, so you can take out the garbage. This reminds me of the old song written by Hank Williams, Sr. called "I Saw the Light": "I saw the light, I saw the light, no more darkness, no more night. Now I'm so happy, no sorrow in sight; praise the Lord, I saw the light." Whatever you feed (light or dark) will fill your house. Let the Lord take the trash out and expel that darkness. He can and he is willing.

The spiritual hosts of wickedness in heavenly places refer to demonic plots, planned and executed in high places. It also refers to spiritual fakes and unclean spirits that we deal with daily. "Demon" means "to torment the mind" and that's what these little flies do. There are many low-ranking demons operating in this area. The other side of this is the Devil wants to orchestrate events that give him credit.

High places are always a place of worship—the very thing the Devil wanted from the beginning. To the Devil, receiving credit for something is worship. When people say things like "the Devil made me do it" about an action they took, the Enemy takes it to himself as praise. Once again, he corrupts and counterfeits. We must begin to take a stand and expose him for the loser he is.

Joseph's life is a great example to us. Joseph could have looked at his life's situation in the natural and with fleshly eyes and blamed the Devil for his situation. He could have given him credit for having him sold as a slave and cast into prison. But Joseph did not. God wasn't done writing Joseph's story and Joseph never left God. What did Joseph say? It's the greatest catchphrase ever: He said people meant it for evil against him, but God meant it for good! He never gave the Enemy a nod of acknowledgement. He focused all his attention on God.

The second battleground after your mind is your heart. Don't forget your heart is also a gateway. What you take (anger, bitterness, discontent, and most of all hurt) affects your heart.

> Above all else, guard your heart, for everything you do flows from it. (Proverbs 4:23 NIV)

> Rid yourselves of all the offenses you have committed, and get a new heart and a new spirit. Why will you die, people of Israel? (Ezekiel 18:31 NIV)

> Each tree is recognized by its own fruit. People do not pick figs from thornbushes, or grapes from briers. A good man brings good things out of the good stored up in his heart, and an evil man brings evil things out of the evil stored up in his heart. For the mouth speaks what the heart is full of. (Luke 6:44-45 NIV)

As you see, there is a reason the psalmist prayed for a clean heart and a renewed spirit. He knew the heart was a battleground and that what you took in changed the state of it.

Whatever the state of your heart, God can fix and repair it.

Some of us need a supernatural heart transplant. Some of us need a softened heart. Whatever the state of your heart, God can fix and repair it. You need to begin by putting on your armor of light and breastplate of righteousness. Don't be bitter! Remember this: They didn't wrong you; they wronged God because you belong to him. He will use these situations to mature you and refine you and he will deal with the other person. That's not a battle you are meant to fight.

All sin and garbage fall under one of the categories of the root demons. We must remember that evil spirits like dirt. They are unclean and cannot live in a clean place. Evil spirits root themselves in pride and bitterness, plus other things. The more light (things of God) that you invest in and receive, the harder it is for darkness to creep in. The more we feed the flesh, the easier it is for darkness to come in. The fight doesn't go away, but if we guard our hearts, we will have seasons of peace and seasons of fighting. We will always have a sense of peace even in the hardest battles too because God is ever present with us.

God gives us the ability to overcome anything and be victorious! He gives the instructions, the weapons, and the strategies. He gives us Holy Spirit power and he gives us his authority.

The extent in which we operate in him is our choice. The more we seek him and his ways, the more we will grow, and the more we can do. In the Bible, even Peter's shadow healed people. Isn't that amazing? We can do the same. But first we must take out the garbage and clean house. We need to break generational curses off our families too—every kind, from alcoholism to the occult. It can stop with us through our heavenly Father.

It's time to let it go and move on. We aren't who we used to be. We know better now. God has been showing us his light. Don't ignore it. Be one of those that—through Christ—changes themselves, and then changes their families. Let's be those who hunger and thirst for him and his ways. Let's be those (like so many others in the Bible) who live without compromise. We have compromised with the world long enough. It's time to take out the trash of this world and replace it with more of God. I want more of him, and I'm sure you do too. I want to stand in my promised land and reign in victory!

12

Be a Gatekeeper

A gate allows entry and exit to and from a place. In the Bible, cities had gates and those gates had gatekeepers. The gatekeeper's job was to control the flow in and out of the city, and to make sure the right people came in and the wrong people did not. Lots of business deals were made at the city gates. Men of influence hung around the gates. Where did Boaz go to make the deal to marry Ruth? The gate of the city.

A gate is like a door or an entryway. Things go in and out through them. We are not totally unfamiliar with gates in this modern era, but we have lost the meaning of how gates functioned in Bible times. Most of us don't even realize the power and influence of our gates! We must remember that the concepts in the Bible are still true today. They still stand and they're powerful. We can say that the idea of gates does not fit our era, but the truth is that we simply don't apply the idea as we ought. That's why it is more important now than ever before that we understand our gateways.

Our homes and our cars have doors on them. When you get out of the car or when you are leaving your home (or even going to bed for the night), you secure your property by locking the doors. Why? To keep enemies and thieves out! Gates represent "authority, power, and influence." In the Bible, gates were used primarily for protection. They were open during the day and closed at night.[19]

---

19. James Strong, "G4439 - Pylē - Strong's Greek Lexicon (KJV)," Blue Letter Bible, accessed May 31, 2022, https://www.blueletterbible.org/lexicon/g4439/kjv/tr/0-1/.

What we let into our gates is going to influence us and can lead to giving wrong things power and influence in our lives. Think of it this way. If all we hear, speak, and see is darkness and evil, they will be our primary influence: the world and sin. If we are speaking Christ, listening to Christlike conversations, and looking at things God's way, he will be our influence. Light expels darkness, so the more we take in God's things, the less we let the world into our gates. However, too often we leave our spiritual gates wide open. Why do we do this? I truly believe the answer is an easy one.

What we let into our gates is going to influence us and can lead to giving wrong things power and influence in our lives.

We have become ignorant to the Enemy's devices over time. We no longer even realize how important our gateways are or how they work! The Devil likes to make important things of no importance.

> If you do well, shall you not be accepted? But if you do not do well, sin is crouching at the door. It desires to dominate you, but you must rule over it." (Genesis 4:7 MEV)

Sin is literally waiting at your door. I love this translation because it makes it clear that sin literally wants to dominate us. The definition of "dominate" is to "have a commanding influence on; exercise control over."[20] Sin is lying in wait for you. Picture a crouching lion, belly to the ground and every muscle taut, ready to pounce on its prey. Peter warned that the Enemy is like a lion seeking whom he may devour in 1 Peter 5:8, so it should be no surprise that sin wants to dominate us and is crouching at the door. It wants to take over and rule us.

---

20. "Dominate Definition & Meaning," Merriam-Webster (Merriam-Webster), accessed May 31, 2022, https://www.merriam-webster.com/dictionary/dominate.

We have three major gateways, and the Enemy is constantly trying to gain access and use them against us. What are they? Our eyes, ears, and mouth! Those are three physical ones, but there's also the gateways of our mind and heart. Your five senses can also be gateways, but what we see, what we hear, and what we speak are our three major ones. There is a Japanese proverb called the three wise monkeys: One monkey is covering his eyes, another his ears, and the last one, his mouth: see no evil, hear no evil, and speak no evil. Although it originated in Japan, it was further elaborated on by Confucius and gradually made its way to Europe and was considered a serious call to purity.

It's no wonder the Enemy uses these gateways. We are always watching, listening, or speaking, yet we are often deceived into thinking that none of these things matter much in our modern lives. *They are NO big deal* we tell ourselves, but we are wrong. So where should we begin? At the beginning, of course!

Now the serpent was more crafty than any other beast of the field that the Lord God had made. He said to the woman, "Did God actually say, 'You shall not eat of any tree in the garden'?" And the woman said to the serpent, "We may eat of the fruit of the trees in the garden, but God said, 'You shall not eat of the fruit of the tree that is in the midst of the garden, neither shall you touch it, lest you die.'" But the serpent said to the woman, "You will not surely die. For God knows that when you eat of it your eyes will be opened, and you will be like God, knowing good and evil." So when the woman saw that the tree was good for food, and that it was a delight to the eyes, and that the tree was to be desired to make one wise, she took of its fruit and ate, and she also gave some to her husband who was with her, and he ate. Then the eyes of both were opened, and they knew that they were naked. And they sewed fig leaves together and made themselves loincloths. And they heard the sound of the Lord God walking in the garden in the cool of the day, and the man and his wife hid themselves from the presence of the Lord God among the trees of the garden. But the Lord God called to the man and said to him, "Where are you?" And he said, "I heard the sound of you in the garden, and I was afraid, because I was naked, and I hid myself." He said, "Who told you that you were naked? Have you eaten of the tree of which I commanded you not to eat?" The man said, "The woman whom you gave to be with me, she gave me fruit of the tree, and I ate." Then the Lord God said to the woman, "What is this that you have done?" The woman said, "The serpent deceived me, and I ate." (Genesis 3:1-13 ESV)

Immediately the Enemy, the old serpent, was talking to the woman, and she is listening! He asked her what God had told her first thing. He was very subtle. The meanings of the word *subtle* include "clever and indirect; disguised in purpose" as well as "artful and crafty."[21] He came at her all sly and smooth, so as not to raise any alarm. Depicting the Devil as a big red man with horns, a tail, and a pitchfork has done a disservice to us all. He is sly and smooth and presents himself as the very thing you think you want and need. The Bible describes him before the fall as perfect in beauty, and it says, in the New Testament, that he can disguise himself as an angel of light. So here he comes, a smooth operator, and immediately asks Eve a question. He gets her listening, and she gives him her ear. The last thing we want to do is give our ear to the wrong person or thing.

Satan asked, "Has God said, you shall not eat of any tree of the garden?" In truth, God did not directly tell Eve; Adam told Eve. This left room for Eve to question the directive, if pressure was applied in the right spot. Trust me, when I say the Enemy always knows the target, he really does. We must be walking in God's ways and be wise to the Enemy's tactics.

---

21. "Subtle Definition & Meaning," Merriam-Webster (Merriam-Webster), accessed May 31, 2022, https://www.merriam-webster.com/dictionary/subtle.

God told Adam this:

> And the Lord God commanded the man, saying, "Of every tree of the garden you may freely eat; but of the tree of the knowledge of good and evil you shall not eat, for in the day that you eat of it you shall surely die" (Genesis 2:16-17 NKJV).

According to the chronological order of the story, it's safe to assume the woman had not yet been created when the command was given to Adam. After the command was given, God decided that it was not good for man to be alone, and he created Eve. Nowhere in scripture, apart from Eve's later dialogue with the serpent, do we see God give that command again. However, Eve knew about it.

"And the woman said…" Eve is now speaking to the serpent; she has used her second gateway: her mouth! She is now in a dialogue with the Enemy. Don't you want to scream, "No, Eve, run away and rebuke that dirty snake; be wise, Eve!" But the truth is that in our modern time, we are still falling for this same trick—hook, line, and sinker. Satan doesn't need new tricks and traps when we are still falling into the old ones!

In verses 2-3, Eve tells him that God said they can eat of all trees *but* the tree of knowledge of good and evil, and she continues with, "God has said 'You will not eat of it, *nor will you touch it*, or else you will die'" (MEV).

God's command was to not *eat* it only. There was nothing said about touching it. We could justify this in our heads in many ways. Maybe she thought that in order to eat it you had to touch it, or that this approach was for the best because if she thinks she can't even touch it, she will stay away from it altogether. Regardless of how we justify it, it does not take away the fact that God's command had been twisted. This created an area of confusion for the serpent to exploit. This should be a sobering lesson for us on entertaining a dialogue with the Enemy. Whether it was Adam that added it in his effort to keep Eve away from the tree or not, we can see that just a small deviation from the truth can be deadly. Satan, after all, is the father of lies; and when he speaks a lie, he is speaking his native language.[22] The best thing to do is not entertain him. We should not open our gateway unless we are commanding him to leave.

In the next section the serpent speaks. He has her full attention. Eve opened her gateways, and their conversation is really flowing. The Devil starts out simply by saying, "Hey, can I ask you a question?" Eve feels comfortable talking to him, and he is getting ready to make his move. Have you ever experienced this in life? You go somewhere with your Christian guard up, knowing to watch your conversations and keep your witness. Therefore, you stick to small talk, just insignificant conversation. After a while, you get comfortable and realize you have engaged in conversations you should not have had. Satan tells Eve that she will not die. Then he suggests that God was, in fact, holding out on her and Adam. Satan tells Eve that God knew that if they ate of the tree their eyes would be open, and they would be like God, knowing good and evil.

With his first question, Satan planted a seed of doubt using her ears when he questions thus, "Has God said?" Now he is moving full speed: "You can eat, and you won't die. In fact, you could be like God!" It's okay. God just doesn't want you to be like him. The Enemy is the prince of the air, and don't think he doesn't try to get you twisted in your thinking by twisting words as they enter your ears. This entangles you as it coils around you. The serpent heard God's command, so he planned and executed a method that would twist that same command so he could deceive Eve. Eve might have already had her suspicions; we don't know what she was thinking. She was not there when God gave the command. Possibly she had doubts. If this was not the case, why did the serpent not go to Adam first instead? The serpent could not go to Adam because the serpent knew that the only way to get to a man was through his wife. Ladies, I encourage you to not be the thing that causes your house to fall. *Guard your gateways!*

---

22. See John 8:44.

In verse 6, the woman *saw* that the tree was good! She had listened, she had spoken, and now she was looking and realized that it was pleasing to the eyes! It pleased her eyes! There are no records indicating that this tree was more beautiful than all the rest, but this is proof that the Enemy can even dress up death with his lies. If we do not protect our gateways, we will fall for this trap every time. Even today, they make everything they want to sell appealing to your eyes. They dress mannequins prettily so you will buy the outfit. They bring out the most luscious desserts so you will see them. If you watch shows about restaurants, they talk about the colors and the climate and the décor, as their goal is to make your experience aesthetically pleasing to your eyes to draw you in.

Eve is looking at this tree now like the cover of a magazine. It pleased her eyes and she desired it. So, *crunch!* She ate it and shared it with her husband!

When we open our doors to the Enemy, it's not only ourselves that get attacked.

Satan didn't have to enter Adam's gateways because he had already infiltrated Eve's, and she shared the fruit with her husband! *But!* If Adam had been doing his job as a proper gatekeeper over the garden over which he had dominion, would the serpent have had all this time to enter Eve's gates? When we open our doors to the Enemy, it's not only ourselves that get attacked. We bring our family and friends along without even realizing it. Not only do we eat of the sin, but we feed our family with it too. Don't get me wrong, Eve is not blameless, but neither is Adam. He should have been protecting his domain from the dirty snake, but that's another lesson, and we are looking at the gateways.

The Bible also says that Eve gave the fruit of the tree to her husband, and he ate. Once her guard was down and she ate, she walked over to Adam and his gateways failed him too. I can almost picture my husband telling me it wasn't my fault, and that he trusted me (because he does).

He believes what I tell him. I am a gatekeeper for my family: my husband and my kids! And so are you—to the family and friends around you! It is time to be the gatekeeper you were called to be, and it is time to shut the gates to the Enemy.

I know we aren't in the garden anymore, but our Enemy only changes tactics when he fails, and this tactic of using our gateways is alive and well. Let's look at this in the natural for a minute. We've all seen department stores with working models. They wear the clothes they want you to buy because they appeal to your eyes. They have music playing to please your ears as you shop. Many of these stores don't sell larger sizes because they don't want fat people wearing their clothes. Why is that? They don't want their clothing to look unappealing, and they think that would happen if they were seen on a larger person. They use your gateways to get you in there and distract you so you will spend more money.

A lot of what we wear or eat is determined by whether they look or smell good. You do not buy a perfume or cologne if it smells bad; the only reason you choose it in the first place is because the scent is sweet, and the bottle is pretty. The Lord gave us our gateways to protect us: if food smells gross, we don't eat it because it would make us sick. If we see something dangerous happening, we can take action to stop it. It's no surprise that Satan twists the things that God gave us as protections to harm us instead. He likes to twist the things of God and he likes to counterfeit them.

Satan wants to appeal to our gateways, so we will be distracted from God's Word, God's Spirit, and our relationship with God. Satan knows that if we are focused on the kingdom and the Word, we are powerful! He knows that when we are focused, we fight smarter and, stronger, and get victory. He knows that when we are focused on the power and might of God, we are not focused on our circumstances, no matter how big the storm around us.

Imagine this scenario: You come home from church where the Spirit was moving strongly. It was an amazing time, and you can't stop thinking about it. God is still speaking to you, but you sit down on the couch, grab the remote to the TV, and flick on the latest popular show, and just like that, the Spirit is quenched. TV is a great distraction to our eye and ear gateways. Shows are made with strong political and social agendas with plenty of shock value to boot. We fall in this trap often.

We start a new show and then halfway through a season, the gay or lesbian romance begins. Perhaps a married character begins a relationship with a person not their spouse. The new character in your favorite show is an atheist or maybe a Buddhist and we learn all about their beliefs, or possibly there will be a Muslim. Or maybe it's something else just as bad. However, there won't be a Christian portrayed, at least not in a good light. Why? Because they are desensitizing our eye gateway, little by little, to the point that believers are no longer embarrassed to recommend filthy shows!

We must protect what we are seeing. Instead, we will tell ourselves that Christian films are rife with poor acting and B-list celebrities. Meanwhile, these movies feed our soul and not our flesh. They focus our eyes on Christ, not on sin, lust, witchcraft, adultery, and gosh knows what else.

The entertainment industry is desensitizing our children, and indoctrinating them, even toddlers. We should watch everything our kids watch because we are not supposed to be ignorant of the Enemy's devices. We know the power and influence of the gateways. Just this year *Muppet Babies* had Gonzo cross-dressing as a princess and saying he was scared people wouldn't like him for being himself.[23] *Blue's Clues* had a pride parade sing-along special with a famous drag queen,[24] and *My Little Pony*[25] on Netflix now includes a lesbian couple. It may be in small bits here and there, but they are planting seeds in our children's gateways—seeds that could lead our children to think the Bible is

23. Muppet Babies, "Gonzo-rella," *Disney Jr.* video, July 23, 2021, https://disneynow.com/shows/muppet-babies.

24. Blue's Clues, "Pride Parade Sing-along with Nina West," *YouTube* video, May 28, 2021, https://www.youtube.com/watch?v=d4vHegf3WPU.

25. My Little Pony, "The Last Crusade," *Netflix* video, June 15, 2019, https://www.netflix.com/browse/genre/783.

wrong and this stuff is okay. They really wanted to cancel *Bluey* because it was too wholesome and not diverse enough. It's for toddlers! If your kids are watching, you need to do the same. You are their gatekeeper, and until they are old enough, you are their spiritual head and spiritually responsible for them.

> *"The eye is the lamp of the body.* If your eyes are healthy, your whole body will be full of light. But if your eyes are unhealthy, your whole body will be full of darkness. If then the light within you is darkness, how great is that darkness!" (Matthew 6:22-23 NIV, emphasis mine)

> I will not *look with approval* on anything that is vile. (Psalm 101:3 NIV, emphasis mine)

Our eyes are important. In Genesis 3:6, the word for "saw" has the same root word[26] translated "turned their eyes" in Isaiah 17:7, which means "to perceive, consider, inspect and behold with intention and purpose."[27] The Enemy wants to define and frame what we are beholding with our eyes when our eyes should be on the prize: the kingdom of God.

Let's Talk About Our Ears

What we hear is important. It enters our mind and heart. Have you ever fallen asleep with the TV on only to wake in the middle of the night in a hot blinding sweat and your heart racing from a nightmare? You fell asleep watching an action film, and now robots are attacking you in your dreams. As you wake up, you glance at the TV only to discover that your innocent program had turned into a horror movie while you slept. The sound of that movie entered your ears, made its way to your brain, and your body took it right in and responded. Our ears are open gates. We

26. James Strong, "7200. Raah," Strong's Hebrew: 7200. רָאָה (Raah) -- to see, accessed May 31, 2022, https://biblehub.com/hebrew/7200.htm.

27. James Strong, "8159. Shaah," Hebrew Concordance: Yiš·'eh -- 2 occurrences, accessed May 31, 2022, https://biblehub.com/hebrew/yisheh_8159.htm.

must protect them: ours and our families' ears. I've made it a habit of going to sleep to a reading of Psalm 91 for this reason.

It's equally important to consider what we are saying to the little ears around us. If I tell my twins they are stupid and good for nothing, I'm planting that seed in their minds. The Enemy can (and will) use that against them later. Similarly, if I teach them Scripture and about God's love, they will be able to use that against the Enemy when he tries to lie to them.

I remember the nurses in the NICU when they were born telling us about wimpy, white boys and how they are the lowest on the totem pole and do the worst at getting home and surviving. When my good friend and kingdom connection, Lisa Hicks, heard them speaking, she turned on her feet and told the woman not to say that again. Then she went to each boy and told them they were mighty warrior boys instead. Why? As you will learn, what we hear and speak is important.

> So then faith comes by *hearing,* and hearing by the word of God. (Romans 10:17 NKJV, emphasis mine)

> He who has *ears to hear*, let him hear! (Matthew 11:15 NKJV, emphasis mine)

> Give ear, O my people, to my law*; incline your ears* to the words of my mouth. (Psalm 78:1 NKJV, emphasis mine)

Obedience is the result of attentive hearing and conscious listening.

Our ears need to be tuned to God's voice and God's Word. What goes into our ears eventually comes out! Hearing is a foundational stone of obedience. The Hebrew word for obey is *shama* which means "to hear intelligently, to listen and give heed."[28] The Greek word obey or obedience is *hupakoe*, which means "hear under."[29] Obedience is the result of attentive hearing and conscious listening.

> But He said, "More than that, blessed are those *who hear* the word of God and keep it!" (Luke 11:28 NKJV, emphasis mine)

The other thing we listen to with our ears is music. Lucifer was the chief musician before he was thrown down from heaven, so he knows the importance of music.

> You were in Eden, the garden of God; Every precious stone was your covering: The sardius, topaz, and diamond, beryl, onyx, and jasper, sapphire, turquoise, and emerald with gold. *The workmanship of your timbrels and pipes was prepared for you on the day you were created.* (Ezekiel 28:13 NKJV, emphasis mine)

Timbrels were the same instrument Miriam used to worship the Lord when they were delivered from Egypt.

Satan knows how music enters our ears and our spirits. He knows how music stirs our soul. This fact explains why much of our music today is filled with filth. We all know songs whose lyrics are vulgar. What's sad is that these songs often become number one hits, so they get a lot of airtime. I cannot even stand to listen to half the artists out there anymore. They are not even hiding that they are in contracts with the Enemy. They put satanic emblems in their videos, talk openly about Satan, use anti-Christian lyrics, and still people say stupid things like, "Just because they worship Satan doesn't mean their songs are *bad*! Doesn't it though? What you believe and serve is an influence in your

---

28. James Strong, "8085. Shama," Strong's Hebrew: 8085. שָׁמַע (shama) -- to hear, accessed May 31, 2022, https://biblehub.com/hebrew/8085.htm.

29. James Strong, "5218. Hupakoé," Strong's Greek: 5218. ὑπακοή (hupakoé) -- obedience, accessed May 31, 2022, https://biblehub.com/greek/5218.htm.

life. What you believe is reflected in what you do! Remember that gates represent authority and influence!

I was recently googling lyrics to old songs that I listened to as a teenager. I sang the songs without a second thought, and boy, let me tell you how easily we sing without paying regard to the words. At one point, I looked over at my husband and said, "Did you know it said this?" Some of them were obvious. How did we not notice? Others was more subtle and kind of sneaky. You can find non-Christian, even anti-Christian, lyrics in everything from John Lennon to Lady Gaga. The truth is we get so obsessed with the trends and so-called legends of this world that we don't bother to pay attention. Then there are the just plain filth songs. If it drops the f- bomb enough, eventually you will sing it and then you will say it.

Let's look at God's music. It carries his anointing. When we praise and worship, it heals and frees us. It propels us closer to the Father and it's good for the soul. Psalm 22:3 says that God inhabits the praises of his people. Worship music sets an atmosphere in your spirit, your home, your car. The Enemy cannot stand to be around it. Psalm 100:4 says "we enter his gates with thanksgiving, and into his courts with praise" (KJV). Yet when we ride around listening to gangster rap, we get filled with a foul language mouth and a tough attitude. It's no wonder that most heavy metal fans are mad all the time and don't know why. There are some rap artists and heavy metal artists whose lyrics and music glorify God, but that just goes to show you the power of music and the effect it has. It will either fill you up with good spiritually or fill you up with worldly garbage.

There are actual scientific studies that show that what you listen to affects your brain, mood, and behavior. There is a sound that a synthesizer makes that sounds like that New Age crystal, which has been proven to stimulate your brain and make you feel a certain way.

They studied people listening to classical music, and it showed a correlation with depression and emotional instability. Beethoven was known to have periods of mania and suffer from depression. Should we be surprised that the state they composed their music in comes out? Music was even shown to affect the behaviors of the listeners.

A paper published in 2003 in *The Journal of Personality and Social Psychology* reported that music can incite aggressive thoughts and feelings. During five experiments with 75 female and 70 male college students, those who heard a violent song were shown to feel more hostile than those who heard a nonviolent song, from the same artist and style.[30] Music has been known to even make you walk faster at the gym, spin harder in spin class, or shop longer in a store. The point is this it stimulates your gateway, and it always has a purpose. So, choose carefully what goes in your ear gate!

Be careful what—and who—you let in your hearing gateway!

A man has joy by the answer of his *mouth,* and a word *spoken* in due season, how good it is! (Proverbs 15:23 NKJV, emphases mine)

The words of a man's *mouth* are deep waters; the wellspring of wisdom is a flowing brook. (Proverbs 18:4 NKJV, emphasis mine)

Death and life are in the power of the *tongue,* and those who love it will eat its fruit. (Proverbs 18:21 NKJV, emphasis mine)

Therefore comfort each other and edify one another, just as you also are doing. (1 Thessalonians 5:11 NKJV)

---

30. Craig A. Anderson, Nicholas L. Carnagey , and Janie Eubanks, "Exposure to Violent Media: The Effects of Songs with Violent Lyrics on ...," apa.org (apa.org), accessed June 1, 2022, https://www.apa.org/pubs/journals/releases/psp-845960.pdf.

Watch your mouth! I'll say it again: Watch your mouth! Our tongue is strong and powerful, yet we get caught up in idle talk and gossip and speak evil over others. We need to zip our lips! If a conversation doesn't build up the body and glorify God, don't agree with it. Speak life to a situation instead and then zip it. The Bible tells us that the tongue must be controlled. We praise the Lord, and later, gossip about someone else's scandal and heartache. This is a great gateway for the Enemy.

There's a saying that "sticks and stones may break my bones, but words will never hurt me." Tell that to the person on the receiving end of those brutal words as they cut deep into their spirit. Today, bullying has emerged as leading factor in the suicide rate. We sometimes treat our cruel words as light jokes, but they are not. They can stir up depression and insecurity and allow the Enemy access into our brains through our hearing gateways. Once in there, he can pump more lies into our brains, and we'll believe them. That song, and many others like it, are chanted like a playground mantra, teaching our kids to harden themselves to the hurt they are experiencing. What? As someone who's had many words slung her way, let me tell you: Words hurt.

They can cut to the very core. There were times I didn't want to leave the house or see people because of how other people spoke to me and my children. The Enemy loves to get us off by ourselves, and people's words can help drive us there.

What we say has consequences.

Words can lead to spiritual bondage in the life of a believer. What we say truly matters. We need to start holding ourselves accountable for the things we say. If we speak life and God's Word, we will build others up and help build a barrier the Enemy cannot penetrate. Think about it. Your words have the capacity to either drive someone over the edge or pull them back to safer ground. Many people's biggest regrets are those awful thing they said to a loved one, that they never got a chance to make right.

When will we learn that we do not have the right to say whatever comes into our mind? What we say has consequences. Did you know that speaking ill over someone is a form of cursing and considered witchcraft? That means that when we say something like I hope he or she gets what's coming to her, you are cursing that person. We choose what we say. We need to weigh what we say.

As we read earlier: "Death and life are in the power of the tongue, and those who love it will eat its fruit" (Proverbs 18:21). That should sober us. Our words have very real power—they carry life and death. We will eat the fruit of what we speak. That is a sobering thought, especially if you have been speaking evil over people and situations. People often use the phrase: "They will get their just desserts." Some of us will definitely not want to eat the dessert created from what we have been speaking. We can't continue to let this gateway run wild.

Posting unkind words on social media is the same as speaking those words. What flows out of you in any way is an extension of your heart and mind. We must remember that social media is a very public platform. We can delete it, but everyone has already seen it and passed it around, so the damage has already been done. The seed has already been planted.

Bullying is one of the worst things you can choose to do with your mouth gate. Too often we make light of it, thinking it helps people develop a thicker skin and a stronger backbone. However, the sad truth is that it doesn't work that way. Recently a little boy who was way too young took his own life because his own family was bullying him. This is not an isolated incident either. Suicide because of bullying is rampant. Words are dangerous. They are like seeds; they can produce health and life or cancer and death.

So, begin to be mindful of your gateways. Pay attention to the gates you have left open and become a good gatekeeper through the power of Christ. Your choice not only affects you, but everyone you love. You have more at stake than you realize. Do not ever believe the lie that it's not that big of a deal. The serpent will always whisper that in our ears, but the more we take heed to wrong ideas, the more we defile our ears, making it harder for us to hear from God. The more we defile our speech, the harder it will be to prophesy and speak for him. The more we defile our eyes, the harder it will be for us to see what the Holy Spirit want us to see. When things become defiled, they become ineffective. Protect your gateways. A good habit is to pray Psalm 141 over yourself regularly.

Lord, I cry out to You; make haste to me! Give ear to my voice when I cry out to You. Let my prayer be set before You as incense, the lifting up of my hands as the evening sacrifice. Set a guard, O Lord, over my mouth; keep watch over the door of my lips. Do not incline my heart to any evil thing, to practice wicked works with men who work iniquity; And do not let me eat of their delicacies. Let the righteous strike me; it shall be a kindness. And let him rebuke me; it shall be as excellent oil; let my head not refuse it. For still my prayer is against the deeds of the wicked. Their judges are overthrown by the sides of the cliff, and they hear my words, for they are sweet. Our bones are scattered at the mouth of the grave, as when one plows and breaks up the earth. But my eyes are upon You, O God the Lord; in You I take refuge; do not leave my soul destitute. Keep me from the snares they have laid for me, and from the traps of the workers of iniquity. Let the wicked fall into their own nets, while I escape safely. (Psalm 141 NKJV)

13

You Have the Right to Remain Silent

Being a Gatekeeper, Part Two

Picture a can of shaving cream. Once you squirt that foam out, you cannot put it back in the can. Our words are like that. Once you say them, you cannot take them back. They have been released, you have sown a seed, and it is only a matter of time until you reap the harvest. The principle of sowing and reaping is straightforward.

> Do not be deceived: God cannot be mocked. A man reaps what he sows. Whoever sows to please their flesh, from the flesh will reap destruction; whoever sows to please the Spirit, from the Spirit will reap eternal life. Let us not become weary in doing good, for at the proper time we will reap a harvest if we do not give up. (Galatians 6:7-9 NIV)

This principle is simple: what we plant, we will harvest. If you were a farmer, you would not plant corn and expect to harvest wheat. The same is true spiritually. We should expect to harvest the seed we have sown into our field of life!

These gateways are vital to our health and well-being. Sometimes we fight battles that could have been avoided, simply by controlling our tongue. Too many of us are not winning our battles and do not know why. However, the answer is clear: We have given our gateways over to the Enemy and have handed him the keys to our gates! What we see, what we hear, what we speak, and everything we let into our hearts, our homes, and our minds plays a significant role in our life. We must become wise to the Enemy's pathways and close our gates to them. We need to examine this, because what we do not know, what we are letting slide, and what we are accepting can and will hurt us.

Remember this: You have the right to remain silent! A popular slogan from government posters during World War II was: "Loose lips sink ships!" The government wanted people to pay attention to what they shared without thinking. The wrong information spoken in the wrong quarter had the capacity to cost American lives. Think about that. How much do you speak without thinking? I remember coming to this realization one day. I was talking to hear myself speak—to fill the void of the quiet. There was a time when quiet made my skin crawl. Now I cherish peace and quiet.

"Loose lips sink ships!"

How often do you gossip about others? How many lies do you think you have told? How often do you speak negatively? Or how often do you speak to fill the silence?

When you type on a word processor, it keeps track of your word count at the bottom of the page. It lets you know exactly how many words you have used and how many pages you have written. I wonder what it would be like if we could see something like that in our life every day. What if we had a record of our many idle and negative words, gossip, unkindness, and filth? How high would our number be? I have a feeling we would be disgusted by the number. I guarantee you would want to change and speak differently if you took a hard look at this. The good news is that we do not have to continue like this anymore. We can change this, and it starts now. *You have the right to remain silent!*

In 1 and 2 Corinthians, Paul wrote about a time in a believer's life when we would have to account for all the things we have said and done. It is not the same as the great white throne judgment when unbelievers are judged. This is called the judgment seat of Christ. We will be in heaven when it happens, and it determines our reward there. Jesus also taught about this in Luke, and it is mentioned in Revelation 22. Our words and deeds matter. If we choose to say and do things that bear good fruit and benefit others instead of choosing to be destructive or idle, we are actively preparing for our future in heaven.

> Then he turned to his host. "When you put on a luncheon or a banquet," he said, "don't invite your friends, brothers, relatives, and rich neighbors. For they will invite you back, and that will be your only reward. Instead, invite the poor, the crippled, the lame, and the blind. *Then at the resurrection of the righteous, God will reward you for inviting those who could not repay you.*" (Luke 14:12-14 NLT, emphasis mine)

> "Look, I am coming soon, *bringing my reward with me to repay all people according to their deeds.* I am the Alpha and the Omega, the First and the Last, the Beginning and the End." (Revelation 22:12-13 NLT, emphasis mine)

> So whether we are here in this body or away from this body, our goal is to please him. For we must all stand before Christ to be judged. *We will each receive whatever we deserve for the good or evil we have done in this earthly body.* (2 Corinthians 5:9-10 NLT, emphasis mine)

> For no one can lay any foundation other than the one already laid, which is Jesus Christ. If anyone builds on this foundation using gold, silver, costly stones, wood, hay, or straw, their work will be shown for what it is, *because the Day will bring it to light. It will be revealed with fire,* and *the fire will test the quality of each person's work. If what has been built survives, the builder will receive a reward.* If it is burned up, the builder will suffer

loss *but yet will be saved* —even though only as one escaping through the flames. (1 Corinthians 3:11–15 NIV, emphases mine)

We need to build the foundation of our words on gold, silver, and costly stones. Yes, we are saved through faith, so this is not that type of judgment. Our words and deeds will be put to trial in the end. Will yours burn away in the flames? Or will they withstand the heat?

Loose lips undeniably sink ships, especially our spiritual ships. Have you ever played the game Battleship? I remember playing with my mom as a kid. You place your five ships on the board and take turns calling out the coordinates on your grid, until you sink all the other person's ships. We play this game spiritually all the time. We have spiritual ships carrying our promises and breakthroughs. As they go through life, we have a choice. We can speak terrible things that will be like torpedoes that speed through the water and hit our ships, until we lose our last one. Or not. The strange thing is that in the end, we are often standing there wondering why our ship sank, when it was the direct result of our own speech! We must learn that our loose lips sink our own ships.

Death and life are in the power of the tongue, and those who love it will eat its fruits. (Proverbs 18:21 ESV)

The NLT renders it this way:

The tongue can bring death or life; those who love to talk will reap the consequences.

Not only will we eat the fruit of our tongues, but we will reap the consequences. Remember the principle of reaping and sowing? It applies to our words too. Trust me when I say that the last thing you want to do is survey your fruit at harvest time and see that you have reaped the consequences of your idle speech. That is not what I want, and I am sure that it is not what you want either. We must change our ways. There was once a chewing gum commercial that claimed to clean up a dirty mouth.

A person might be covered in mud, but because they chewed that gum, their mouth was sparkling clean. Wouldn't it be nice if it were that easy? The truth is that changing our ways of speech requires discipline.

Discipline refers to "control that is gained by insisting that rules be followed" and "strict training that corrects or strengthens" as well as "habits and ways of acting that are gotten through practice." The verb means to "train in self-control or obedience" and "to bring under control."[31] In other words, practice makes perfect. You need to practice over and over again until you have better control. Did you know that anything you practice for three weeks becomes a new habit? We must form new habits in our speech. Daily practice in training and disciplining our words to line up with the Father's will change us.

> When there are many words, sin is unavoidable, but the
> one who controls his lips is prudent. (Proverbs 10:19)

This scripture is a warning about speaking too much. It screams caution. Beware! There's trouble ahead! The more words you use, the greater the capacity for sin that you open. Zip the lip and avoid the trap!

We are praying and warring; we are fighting for miracles and breakthroughs, so if we are speaking death and curses in our lives or the lives of others, we will not be effective. When we speak evil or negatively over someone's life, we are using witchcraft. Witchcraft has no place in the kingdom of God. Be aware of what you are saying, and how you say it! There is power in your words.

As a child, I was repeatedly told that if I did not have anything good to say, I should not say anything at all! What a pearl of wisdom! I never realized how important this was until I grew up. We do not have to say everything that pops into our minds, and we do not have to share everything on social media either. There is no difference between texting or posting on social media and speaking. They are all forms of communication and an outlet for our thoughts. What we put there matters. Too

---

31. "Discipline Definition & Meaning," Merriam-Webster (Merriam-Webster), accessed June 1, 2022, https://www.merriam-webster.com/dictionary/discipline.

often those areas are dismissed as not the same as actual speech and considered an easy pass to sin. The world would have you think that you can say anything on social media, but we will answer and account for every word spoken, and that includes every word we type and every status we post. That is why personal discipline is vital.

> He who guards his mouth preserves his life, but
> he who opens wide his lips will have destruction.
> (Proverbs 13:3 MEV)

We know that if we guard something, we must watch over it carefully and protect it from harm. We must use wisdom. Cities had gatekeepers at the gates and watchmen on the walls. They protected and watched over them diligently. In like fashion, we must become gatekeepers and watchmen over our own lives and borders, as well as those of our spouses and children. How can we train them to be good gatekeepers, if we have abandoned our posts, leaving them unprotected? We must train ourselves, so we can train the future generations. We must be the example of what we want to see! The Bible also tells us to "train up a child in the way they should go" (Proverbs 22:6 ESV). We cannot train anyone in anything we do not understand. How can you teach a lesson that you, yourself, never learned? You cannot!

> Finally, brothers and sisters, whatever is true, whatever is
> honorable, whatever is right, whatever is pure, whatever
> is lovely, whatever is commendable, if there is any
> excellence and if anything worthy of praise, think about
> these things. (Philippians 4:8 NASB)

This verse should be the filter that strains our words. To take control of our words, we must first take control of our thoughts because "out of the abundance of the heart his mouth speaks" (Luke 6:45 NKJV).

> "Either make the tree good and its fruit will be good or
> make the tree bad and its fruit will be bad; for a tree is

known by its fruit. Brood of vipers! How can you speak good things when you are evil? For the mouth speaks from the overflow of the heart. A good person produces good things from his storeroom of good, and an evil person produces evil things from his storeroom of evil. I tell you that on the day of judgement people will have to account for every careless word they speak. For by your words you will be acquitted, and by your words you will be condemned." (Matthew 12:33-37)

Technically our thoughts our hearts and our speech are connected. They are different gateways to the same city, and those gates lead to our inner man. Our mouth speaks our thoughts and what is in our hearts—good or bad. Changing our hearts is the key to disciplining our mouths. If we address the state of our heart, it will change our speech. What does the Word say? I know we have mentioned it before, but this is important: "Create in me a clean heart, O God; and renew a right spirit within me." (Psalm 51:10 KJV). This should be our prayer. May God constantly show us what is dirty in our hearts and our lives, and may we allow the Holy Spirit to cleanse us. Remember that commercial? Got a dirty mouth? Clean it up with the Holy Spirit!

Changing our hearts is the key to disciplining our mouths.

In the passage above, the word "careless" in Matthew 12:36 is rendered "idle" in other translations. "Idle" means "having no employment, inactive, lacking worth or basis, vain, shiftless, and lazy."[32] This means we should be the opposite. We should speak with great purpose and use our mouth for the good things of the Lord. We should not just allow ourselves to spew forth words without purpose, words that have no point and are unprofitable in our lives and unprofitable to the kingdom.

---

32. "Idle Definition & Meaning," Merriam-Webster (Merriam-Webster), accessed June 1, 2022, https://www.merriam-webster.com/dictionary/idle.

Hidden in Plain Sight: Identifying Our Little Foxes

Mark 8:36 says this: "For what shall it profit a man if he gains the whole world, and loses his own soul?" (NKJV) How sad! To have the best of material things but lose our soul. This takes us back to the judgment seat of Christ. All earthly gains amount to ash in the end—useless fruitless things that add nothing to our eternity. We have taken our salvation and the Bible too lightly for far too long. We need to have an eternal perspective while we live our earthly lives. God instructs us and disciplines us because he loves us. He teaches us these lessons, so we can be effective witnesses, not just in our speech but also in our lifestyle choices. It is time to get serious and quit playing games with our salvation and our walk. Our eternal life depends on it!

> For the Lord disciplines the one he loves, and chastises
> every son whom he receives. (Hebrews 12:6 ESV)

If you are going to speak, speak what is useful and do it with wisdom. Make sure your words bring life and edification to the body, not death, destruction, and misery. Speak life! Let your mouth be like a refreshing spring.

> Therefore encourage (admonish, exhort) one another and
> edify (strengthen and build up) one another, just as you
> are doing. (1 Thessalonians 5:11 AMPC)

The word "therefore" tells us that we need to read what was written before it. It is a conjunction that looks backward, so we can properly look forward and understand the next section. Anytime you read "therefore" at the beginning of a verse, it's continued from the section before it. They go together. I encourage you to read all of 1 Thessalonians 5 in the AMPC translation, but for the sake of the "therefore" here are a few verses of it:

> For God has not appointed us to [incur His] wrath [He
> did not select us to condemn us], but [that we might]
> obtain [His] salvation through our Lord Jesus Christ

(the Messiah) Who died for us so that whether we are still alive or are dead [at Christ's appearing], we might live together with Him and share His life. Therefore encourage (admonish, exhort) one another and edify (strengthen and build up) one another, just as you are doing. (1 Thessalonians 5:9-11 AMPC)

Compared to the rest of us, our mouth is small, and our tongue is just a small muscle compared to the rest of our muscles. But our tongue and our mouth have a great deal of physical strength and dexterity because we use them constantly. Of course, some of that is necessary, but we need to learn to value quiet. This passage encourages us to exhort and edify one another. That's one of the purposes for our ability to speak. However, if we are using it for evil instead of good, the Enemy sits back and watches. He has no need to do anything if we are attacking one another. If we do that, we disqualify ourselves. If someone calls me for advice, what proceeds out of my mouth can edify them and lead them to God's ways or pump them full of evil and send them on the wrong path following worldly ways.

There is more power than we realize in what we say. We should not blame the Devil for our own actions. Yes, he can influence us, and our flesh is naturally evil, but we are responsible for our own choices. Harnessing this isn't something we can do on our own. We must ask the Lord to help us and allow the Holy Spirit to do a work in us. We need his help, but we must start taking responsibility for our own actions.

> For I know that nothing good dwells in me, that is, in my flesh. For I have the desire to do what is right, but *not the ability to carry it out.* (Romans 7:18 ESV, emphasis mine)

> For the *desires of the flesh are against the Spirit,* and the desires of the Spirit are against the flesh, for these are opposed to each other, to keep you from doing the things you want to do. (Galatians 5:17 ESV, emphasis mine)

We need to discern when we should speak and when we should remain silent. Sometimes the wisest thing to do is zip thy lip. If we do not know what to say, we shouldn't say anything at all. Do not speak just to respond. It's okay to not have an answer. In fact, not knowing gives us an opportunity to pray with someone to seek advice from the one who has *all* the answers.

Ecclesiastes 3:7 says there is "a time to tear and a time to mend, a time to be silent and a time to speak" (NIV). When we learn when to be silent and when to speak, we are more effective. James 1:19 says to be "quick to listen, slow to speak." Even Jesus needed quiet time alone with God. He had to know when to speak and when to be silent. Sometimes Jesus directed people to not tell others about something he did (Mark 1:43-45), but other times he told them to speak and spread the word. Not everyone listened, but Jesus was using wisdom over his mouth with great purpose! It is also safe to assume he knew Judas would betray him well before the dinner but held that information close until then. Even then, he did not share it with the rest. The way Jesus dealt with Judas is one of the greatest examples of not having an-eye-for-an-eye mentality. It would have been easy to say that Judas deserved it, or that Jesus wanted to show that he knew all along and wasn't a pushover. But Jesus did none of these things. Instead, he used great wisdom and told them only what they needed to know.

We need to learn the need-to-know concept. It is a good thing to get better at, and more familiar with, knowing when to be silent and when to speak. Even the right word at the wrong time can go wrong. Always seek wisdom and follow the Holy Spirit's guidance before you speak. Remember he is the teacher, and you are the student; allow the Spirit to teach and guide you.

When Jesus was on trial, he understood this discipline. He fulfilled a prophecy in doing so.

He was oppressed and He was afflicted, *yet He opened not His mouth;* He was led as a lamb to the slaughter, and as a sheep before its shearers is silent, *so He opened not His mouth.* (Isaiah 53:7 NKJV, emphases mine)

Now Jesus stood before the governor. And the governor asked Him, saying, "Are You the King of the Jews?" Jesus said to him, "It is as you say." And while He was being accused by the chief priests and elders, *He answered nothing.* Then Pilate said to Him, "Do You not hear how many things they testify against You?" *But He answered him not one word,* so that the governor marveled greatly. (Matthew 27:11-14 NKJV, emphases mine)

Even in our silence, we must use wisdom.

The one who has knowledge restrains his words, and one who keeps a cool head is a person of understanding. *Even a fool is considered wise* when he keeps silent—discerning, when he seals his lips. (Proverbs 17:27-28, emphasis mine)

Discernment is key. There are going to be times when we should speak out but are afraid. Too often we think too much about what others are going to think if we speak, but we need to be more concerned about what our heavenly Father thinks if we do not. Silence is wisdom when it is Spirit-led, but foolish when done in the flesh.

For if you remain completely silent at this time, relief and deliverance will arise for the Jews from another place, but you and your father's house will perish. Yet who knows whether you have come to the kingdom for such a time as this?" (Esther 4:14 NKJV, emphases mine)

Esther was faced with a decision: speak or be silent. We do have a free will. God created us this way. We can't remain silent when God calls us to speak, or he will raise up someone else to say what he wants to say. However, what if the impact of what you have to say would save your life and the lives of those around you, as in Esther's case? What if it is a pivotal moment in your life? What if this is the moment for which you were created? Perhaps this is the time you have been brought into the kingdom to accomplish. You could have been born at any other time in history, but God chose the here and now for you. You have purpose.

Esther prayed and fasted for three days after this for wisdom and direction. This is a perfect example of how we should approach our choices.

You have purpose.

Imagine that your house is on fire and the heat is searing your skin. Flames are blazing around you, and you have the hose in your hand. The instrument of your present salvation is in your grasp, but the only way it will save you is turning it on. You can point it at the fire all day long, but unless the water comes out, it is useless. It'll burn up along with everything else. This is the same effect your spoken words in prayer have. The Word of God is living water, and it will quench the flames of the Enemy. It is literally a fiery dart extinguisher.

By not speaking and warring in prayer, you are not releasing his words into the atmosphere, which is how you win battles. The Enemy cannot read your mind, so you cannot cast him out with your thoughts. You must open your mouth. Speak it!

> Look at the ships also: though they are so large and are driven by strong winds, they are guided by a very small rudder wherever the will of the pilot directs. So also, the tongue is a small member, yet it boasts of great things. How great a forest is set ablaze by such a small fire! And the tongue is a fire, a world of unrighteousness. The tongue is set among our members, staining the whole body, setting on fire the entire course of life, and set on

fire by hell. For every kind of beast and bird, of reptile and sea creature, can be tamed and has been tamed by mankind, but no human being can tame the tongue. It is a restless evil, full of deadly poison. With it we bless our Lord and Father, and with it we curse people who are made in the likeness of God. From the same mouth come blessing and cursing. My brothers, these things ought not to be so. (James 3:4-10 ESV)

Our tongues can produce water, or they can bring fire. You can either extinguish the flames of hell or help them grow. The choice is truly yours. The Spirit will not force you, he is a gentleman.

We may not be able to bring our speech into absolute perfection, but we can continually submit it to Christ, and he will help us. We can do a better job taming the tongue if we are submitted to the Holy Spirit. We will fall into traps from time to time, but the important thing is to get back up, dust yourself off, and keep practicing. As we grow and change, it will be easier to contain any fire we start. Firemen know how to contain fires and slow the spread of them; they even know how to do controlled fires. In fact, they use them in training. If we follow the Holy Spirit's guidance, we will be able to contain our words a lot better. It is a process, but it is one worth learning.

We have let the Enemy intrude on our gateways for far too long. He tries to convince us that what we say does not matter, that it's no big deal. Even the silly kids' song we mentioned earlier tries to convince us that words do not hurt, but that's not true. The Bible repeatedly warns us about our words and our speech, and teaches us about the power in them, showing us that we need to use wisdom. The Enemy loves to listen to an untamed tongue. He enjoys the havoc and destruction that ensues because of it. It makes his vile job easier. In fact, he can do something else because we are destroying ourselves.

Sometimes our mouths are like the arena in Hunger Games: uncontrolled. We are literally running around taking each other out. When we live our lives cursing, telling dirty jokes, speaking negatively about ourselves and others, murmuring and complaining, gossiping, lying, and the like, we are rooting ourselves into the Enemy's territory deeper with every word. What we speak matters! We just read a proverb a few pages ago that told us that where there are many words, sin was unavoidable. The deeper we allow ourselves to move into the Enemy's territory, the farther we will find ourselves from God's presence. This is why, it is vital that we let the Holy Spirit show us the areas we need to cleanse in ourselves. Our mouths should be used to praise, preach, teach, edify, encourage, pray, speak his Word, and reach the lost. Our mouths should be speaking to our mountains and those belonging to others to bring hope and deliverance. Instead of telling someone how big their giant is, tell the giant how big your God is! Speak life!

If you cannot say something nice today, then you have the right to remain silent. If you do not know what to say, then you have the right to remain silent! If you feel led to speak up by the Spirit, then open your mouth!

Instead of telling someone how big their giant is, tell the giant how big your God is!

Our speech reflects us. Who would even want to hear what we have to say, if we are constantly cursing, gossiping, and spewing filth and garbage? If we spew hate, how can we show God's love and mercy. If we are constantly complaining, how will we be able to tell someone of the goodness of God? What we say matters. We often boldly proclaim how we feel. We can be real Debbie Downers, especially on social media. When we are portraying a Debbie Downer spirit with our words, we are defeating ourselves, and proclaiming that since we are Christians, being in Christ is also a real downer. Because of us, they will never know how good he is in our lives and experience!

This is the crux of the matter: Our words don't just portray who we are, but when we profess Christ, they speak to the whole world about who he is. We need to portray Christ properly!

One of the biggest hurdles we need to face is when others attack us or our family. At that point, we often think we have a right to respond in the same way. We think we are somehow entitled to let the Mama Bear out, because they messed with our cubs. But it's a trap! Too often we fall into it too! When people verbally attack us, it hurts, but that does not give us license to sling it back at them. The best choice we can make is to pray. If we take them to our heavenly Father, he can help us both.

Why should we cause more trouble (and lose good ground we have fought hard to gain), just to sling some dirt back at someone? It's not worth it. The ground we have gained is too valuable.

By retaliating and getting even with someone, we block God from vindicating us. When we take matters out of Christ's hands and put them in our own, we sow seeds we should have not sown, and end up reaping a harvest we will soon regret. Spiritual laws still apply to us, even when we are provoked and our tempers flare. Be assured! The Lord will take care of it! God is our Father, and he will protect his children. He will not allow anyone to get away with anything. For one thing, they will reap the seeds they have sown, and God will deal with them. Truly, he has his hands on both parties, as Job desired in Job 9:33. We can trust him to take care of any problem.

> For we know Him who said, *"Vengeance is Mine, I will repay,"* says the Lord. And again, "The Lord will judge His people." (Hebrews 10:30 NKJV, emphasis mine)

> He permitted no one to do them wrong; yes, *He rebuked kings for their sakes,* saying, "Do not touch My anointed ones, and do My prophets no harm." (Psalm 105:14-15 NKJV, emphasis mine)

> Indeed, this is what the Lord says: "Even the captives of the mighty man will be taken away, and the prey of a tyrant will be rescued; *for I will contend with the*

one who contends with you, and I will save your sons. (Isaiah 49:25 NASB, emphasis mine)

Do not give your gates over to the Enemy just to get even. Remember who fights your battles! It's high time to secure our gates. What goes in will eventually come out. How embarrassed would we be if our children repeated half the stuff we say to our pastor? What if you were dining with the King of Kings? Would your conversation be the same?

Do not lose your good ground for the sake of five minutes of fleshly satisfaction. Nothing is sadder, trust me I know. I have fought the battle of my mouth long and hard. It is not worth it! Hold your tongue and hold your peace. It does not matter what they said to you. They are not justified in saying it, and you will not be justified in your reply either.

> The Lord will fight for you while you [only need to] keep silent and remain calm." (Exodus 14:14 AMP)

You have the right to remain silent! Speak wisely!

14

This Fire Starts at Home

Being a Gatekeeper, Part Three

I baptize you with water for repentance, but he who is coming after me is mightier than I, whose sandals I am not worthy to carry. He will baptize you with the Holy Spirit and fire. (Matthew 3:11 ESV)

For far too long we have been looking for God to strike that match and begin a fire down in our souls. We chase after it. From revival to revival. Outpouring to outpouring. We are always waiting to be burning with the Holy Ghost. We want that beautiful fire to flow strong in us, so that we will walk in a strong anointing and power. I must share a truth with you. This is not about a building or a specific gathering. Fire starts at home. It starts with you, and it starts in your home! Sure, a gathering is refreshing, but if no one shows up with the fire, it's another meeting of the Frozen Chosen Society in there. We must fan our spark into a flame, and that flame into a fire!

Fire starts with you!

The Lord wants to take our fire and start a wildfire! Wildfires often start because of weather conditions. The condition of the environment can cause the fire to spread quickly. Fire needs a lot of fuel to grow.

For example, drought, wind, and extreme temperatures can make a fire larger, faster, and more dangerous. Did you know that the stronger the wind, the faster the fire will spread? Fire needs oxygen to grow, and wind brings an extra air supply to the fire. It flattens the flame, which preheats the fuel and causes spot fires which blow embers and sparks ahead of the main fire into a new source of fuel.

Spiritually, if we want a wildfire to spread amongst us, we must first be set on fire. We must allow the breath of God to blow like a mighty wind over us, spreading the fire, giving life, and understanding, first to ourselves and then to those around us.

> Again He said to me, "Prophesy over these bones and say to them, 'O dry bones, hear the word of the Lord.' Thus says the Lord God to these bones, 'Behold, *I will cause breath* to enter you that you may come to life. I will put sinews on you, make flesh grow back on you, cover you with skin and put breath in you that you may come alive; and you will know that I am the Lord.'" (Ezekiel 37:4-6 NASB1995, emphasis mine)

> But it is a spirit in man, and *the breath of the Almighty* gives them understanding. (Job 32:8 NASB1995, emphasis mine)

> The Spirit of God has made me, and *the breath of the Almighty* gives me life. (Job 33:4 NASB1995, emphasis mine)

Therefore, we must get our conditions ready for that wildfire. Environment is everything. Cacti cannot grow in the tundra, and God cannot flow in certain conditions. There are certain environments He cannot fully move into. I am not putting God in a box of what he can and cannot do. God can always show up and move, but we are talking about creating the perfect environment for a great outpouring, a great and mighty wildfire. Just like that natural wildfire, we are going to need fuel to grow.

Water will still trickle out of a kinked hose, but once you pull it straight and allow the hose to operate as it ought, the water can really flow. It's the same with God. There are certain things that block the Spirit's flow too. Pride is a major one, pride blocks wisdom. The reason we talk a lot about pride in this study is that it is truly destructive and deadly. Therefore, it is crucial that we grasp how to identify it and eradicate it. Pride is the sin that got Lucifer kicked out of heaven.

> But he gives us more grace. That is why Scripture says: *"God opposes the proud* but shows favor to the humble. (James 4:6 NIV, emphasis mine)

> *In his pride* the wicked man does not seek him; in all his thoughts there is no room for God. (Psalm 10:4 NIV, emphasis mine)

> *When pride comes*, then comes disgrace, but with humility comes wisdom. (Proverbs 11:2 NIV, emphasis mine)

> For You save an afflicted and humble people, but bring down those [*arrogant fools*] with haughty eyes. (Psalms 18:27 AMP, emphasis mine)

Just as pride blocks God from imparting deeper heavenly wisdom, greed blocks blessings.

> Whoever *oppresses the poor* shows contempt for their Maker, but whoever is kind to the needy honors God. (Proverbs 14:31 NIV, emphasis mine)

> An inheritance claimed too soon will not be blessed at the end. (Proverbs 20:21 NIV)

> *The greedy* stir up conflict, but those who trust in the Lord will prosper. (Proverbs 28:25 NIV, emphasis mine)

The generous will themselves be blessed, for they share
their food with the poor. (Proverbs 22:9 NIV)

Only the fruit of the Spirit can help spread the fires of revival; the acts of the flesh will have the opposite effect.

Only the fruit of the Spirit can help spread the fires of revival; the
acts of the flesh will have the opposite effect. These are just two examples; I encourage you to go deeper and study how these fleshly choices
taint the environment of God and prevent him from fully moving in a
blazing wildfire.

These *six things the Lord hates*, yes, seven are an
abomination to Him: a proud look, a lying tongue, hands
that shed innocent blood, a heart that devises wicked
plans, feet that are swift in running to evil, a false witness
who speaks lies, and one who sows discord among
brethren. (Proverbs 6:16-19 NKJV, emphasis mine)

God cannot move in conditions that he hates. In order to have the
proper environment, we need to remove these factors from our lives.
First things first, we need to prepare our homes.

One day Elisha went to Shunem. A prominent woman
who lived there persuaded him to eat some food. So
whenever he passed by, he stopped there to eat. Then
she said to her husband, "I know that the one who often
passes by here is a holy man of God, *so let's make* a
small, walled-in upper room and put a bed, a table, a
chair, and a lamp there for him. *Whenever he comes, he
can stay there."* (2 Kings 4:8-10, emphases mine)

Prophets spoke for God and delivered God's message. They were his representatives on earth. I absolutely love this portion of scripture. At every opportunity, this woman brought Elisha into her home and fed him. You can almost picture her sitting with her husband and the prophet at the table, listening to the spoken word. But that was not enough for her. She wanted more! She went a step further and carved out a room for him, so he had a place to reside and dwell whenever he was in the area.

What a lesson can be found in these passages! We must make room for God and give him a place to come and dwell and reside in our home. He is not reserved for Sundays and mid-week services, God is not reserved for the inside of a church. He is not a Sunday God. He is an all-the-time God. We need to bring him home. His dwelling place is within us and our family.

Do you truly bring him home with you? Or do you go home and think you can leave him in the church?

His dwelling place is within us and our family.

Remember the wildfire requires conditions and environments to grow, is your home environment welcoming of his Spirit? Or is it full of language and movies and ways that would grieve him? We cannot stop at preparing our home, we must also prepare our temple!

Don't you know that *your body is a temple* of the Holy Spirit, who is in you, whom you have from God? You are not your own, for you were bought at a price. So glorify God with your body. (1 Corinthians 6:19-20, emphasis mine)

Another translation reads it this way:

What? Do you not know that your body is the temple of the Holy Spirit, who is in you, whom you have received from God, and that you are not your own? You were bought with a price. Therefore glorify God in your body and in your spirit, which are God's. (MEV)

Think about this:

- *God the Father* created our bodies.
- *God the Son* redeemed them.
- *God the Holy Spirit* indwells them.

This makes our body the very temple of the Holy Spirit!

By God choosing the word "temple" to describe the Spirit's dwelling, He conveys that our bodies are the shrine, or the sacred place in which the Spirit not only lives, but is worshiped, revered, and honored. So how we behave, think, and speak, and what we let into our temple through our gateways becomes critically important.

We cannot hide from him or be fake with him. He knows every thought, word, and deed that we use and do. He knows the real us, not just what we show the world, but what our inward man's condition is. He knows the state of our thoughts and our hearts. We need to start preparing and honoring our temples.

Remember the Old Testament? Remember the reverence for the temple? Or even the reverence for him and his Spirit? We need to respect the temple of God with all reverence and honor. We need to glorify God in our body and our spirit. There is a proper way to approach God. When God met with Moses at the burning bush, he said this:

> "Do not come any closer," the Lord warned. "Take off your sandals, for you are standing on holy ground. (Exodus 3:5 NLT)

You have holy ground in you. Are you treating it with reverence?

> The Lord of Heaven's Armies says to the priests: "A son honors his father, and a servant respects his master. *If*

I am your father and master, where are the honor and respect I deserve? You have shown contempt for my name! But you ask, 'How have we ever shown contempt for your name?' You have shown contempt by offering *defiled sacrifices on my altar.* Then you ask, 'How have we defiled the sacrifices?' You defile them by saying the altar of the Lord deserves no respect. When you give blind animals as sacrifices, isn't that wrong? *And isn't it wrong to offer animals that are crippled and diseased?* Try giving gifts like that to your governor, and see how pleased he is!" says the Lord of Heaven's Armies. (Malachi 1:6-8 NLT, emphases mine)

When the Law was given to Moses in the wilderness, the command was to sacrifice only perfect animals. They could not have spot, blemish, wrinkle, or defect. Later in Malachi they were letting unclean dirty things into their temple, and this was God's response.

"How I wish one of you would shut the Temple doors so that these worthless sacrifices could not be offered! I am not pleased with you," says the Lord of Heaven's Armies, "and I will not accept your offerings. *But my name is honored by people of other nations from morning till night.* All around the world they offer sweet incense and *pure offerings* in honor of my name. For my name is great among the nations," says the Lord of Heaven's Armies. *"But you dishonor my name with your actions.* By bringing contemptible food, *you are saying it's all right to defile* the Lord's table. *You say, 'It's too hard to serve the Lord,' and you turn up your noses at my commands,"* says the Lord of Heaven's Armies. "Think of it! Animals that are stolen and crippled and sick are being presented as offerings! Should I accept from you such offerings as these?" asks the Lord. "Cursed is the cheat who promises to give a fine ram from his flock but then sacrifices a

defective one to the Lord. *For I am a great king, "* says the Lord of Heaven's Armies, *"and my name is feared among the nations!"* (Malachi 1:10-14 NLT, emphases mine)

I am convicted just by writing this. I know I have allowed things into my temple that have dishonored my Lord and knowing that my choices have grieved God makes me feel about an inch tall. We cannot bring unclean and disrespectful things into our lives and expect God to move in us the same way he can in other believers who are using their temples as they should. *Lord, please forgive us for every unclean thing we have allowed into our temples. Help us clean house and create an environment that not only pleases you, but always allows the fire of the Holy Spirit to run free.*

But the hour is coming, and is now here, when the true worshipers will worship the Father in spirit and truth, *for the Father is seeking such people to worship him.* God is spirit, and those who worship him must worship in spirit and truth. (John 4:23-24 ESV, emphasis mine)

God is *seeking* those who will worship him "in spirit and truth." I love that. Elsewhere it says that we will find him when we seek him, and we are instructed to seek first his kingdom and his righteousness.

So even though, he tells us to look for him, he is already seeking us. How beautiful. he is such a good Father. Too often, we take him for granted, and yet he seeks those that will be true worshipers.

He is already seeking us.

We worship God based on the truth of who he is, the truth of who we are, the truth of what he does, and the truth of what is going on in our world. We worship with a heart inclined to God and in submission to him. We worship God when our attitudes, actions, and words declare that he is worthy of our praise.

Do our current attitudes, actions, and words testify to others that we worship God? Does our lifestyle point others toward Christ? Or does it point them to the world?

Let's examine the effect of attitudes for a minute. I went through a phase when I believed it was all right for me to have a bad attitude because of something my husband did. That is exactly what I did, and I went with it with everything I had. If I told you the man would just look at me and my temper flared, it would be an understatement. It did not matter where I was or what I was doing either. I was miserable and wanted everyone around me to know it. My husband, on the other hand, was doing everything he could to please me and stay in my good graces. However, I was deeply committed to my "justified" bad attitude. God kept prodding me to ditch it, but I pushed that nudging away. I wanted to dwell there in attitude land. Had I not earned it? Surely my husband deserved this after what he had done. Right? Wrong! My attitude did not only affect me, it also affected my children, the environment in our home and the growth of my marriage, but it didn't stop there. My choice overflowed into my ministry and life outside those relationships too.

My behavior pointed no one to Jesus. I was no use to anyone. If someone had met me on the street at that time, they would not have thought I lived a surrendered life. My attitude caused me to lose good ground. Imagine waking up a year from now, and tracing what you gave up to the Enemy, and what your testimony was like to others. I needed to get an attitude checkup!

Our whole lives should be surrendered in worship to the Father.

Worship is not about music. Worship is our holy response to God, so it includes everything: every choice, every word, the state of our hearts, and every result of our dedication to him. Singing is an overflow of our hearts. He honors that freewill offering by inhabiting us in it, so we use the word "worship" to describe that choice and that part of a church service. (In fact, "worship" as singing in the way it is practiced today only began in the last hundred years. Historically, music was not the focal point of worship. Our actions were.) Our whole lives should be surrendered in worship to the Father.

> The heavens declare the glory of God, and the expanse proclaims the work of his hands. Day after day they pour out speech; night after night they communicate knowledge. There is no speech; there are no words; their voice is not heard. Their message has gone out to the whole earth, and their words to the ends of the world. (Psalm 19:1-4)

Whenever I am feeling stressed or overwhelmed, I sit outside. Sometimes I take my dog with me, so I can go for a walk, but walking or sitting, just being outside always brings me peace. Peace is not found in nature, but it is a side effect of the worship creation is constantly engaged in. It's like listening to everyone singing in church. There's praise all around you, but you must slow down to pay attention to it and sing along. When you are outside, you can join in on it too—and take some lessons from the sunsets and the stars. They speak no words, yet they are continuously worshipping him. Their very existence is an act of worship to him and give him glory. In the same way, our actions should glorify and honor him. Actions speak louder than words.

Fires are just not started. They do not simply appear. You need wood or something dry to burn and you need some flint. In order to get a spark, you must scrape metal against it. Sometimes you get a few sparks that do not give birth to flames and die out in the air before even meeting the kindling, so you might have to do it a few times until that one spark catches and erupts into flames. You need to become the spark that starts the wildfire!

Have you ever been in a meeting when a guest speaker visited that was on a whole other level, spitting straight-truth fireballs? I picture it like when the whirlwind of fire came down and engulfed Elijah before carrying him away. Well, when that guest speaker walks in, you can spiritually see and feel that whirlwind of fire burning in the Holy Spirit. As the Holy Spirit starts to move through the congregation, they catch that fire too. Before you know it, people are dancing in the spirit and moving in his gifts. Breakthroughs mark the fire of the Spirit and the chains of bondage breaking and fall off God's people.

You need to become the spark that starts the wildfire!

However, that speaker did not just turn into a wildfire by stepping into your church and getting behind that pulpit. They had prepared their home and prepared their temple first. They sought Christ, worshiped him, and fellowshipped with him. They had a prayer life and had made room for him in every area of their life. They were a willing vessel. They allowed his holy fire to come into their own sacred and secret places to burn away what was not usable first. They gave in to the process, allowing him to mold them and shape them. There are things in our lives that are not meant to be there. We know about some and are unaware of others, but he knows. When we allow him to sweep through our person with his refining fire to let him remove and burn away those impurities, we will become natural catalysts of his fire too—in ways we could never imagine. Then we can spread his fire to others too.

Let us look at wildfires from a spiritual perspective. What does wind represent in the Word? It represents the Holy Spirit. That means that the stronger the wind, the greater the effect of the Holy Spirit, and the faster the spread of his fire. So, when you are walking around full of fire and the Holy Spirit, you are going to spread it. You can spread it to family, friends, spouses, children, strangers, church—everyone you meet, and before you know it, we have a Holy Ghost wildfire!!

When wildfires spread, they are not isolated to one area or a particular variety of tree. Look at the natural wildfires in California and Oregon, if you do not believe me. They spread and they spread fast.

All it takes is for someone to throw a spark in a dry place and boom, ignition. The same is true for us. If we walk around, sharing that flame with others, we can ignite them as well. God's fire starts spreading, and before you know it, his fire in the spirit is roaring and beautiful. Unlike a natural wildfire, it's not harmful, instead it brings life and health as it refines hearts.

A wildfire of anointing and God's power can burn bigger and faster than we could ever fathom. Isn't that what we want? The Word says that in the last days there will be a great outpouring! Do you want to be a part of it? Do you want to be the one that says, "Here I am, Lord; send me?" I do. I can't think of anything better.

> When the day of Pentecost had arrived, they were all together in one place. Suddenly a sound like that of a *violent rushing wind* came from heaven, and it filled the whole house where they were staying. *They saw tongues like flames of fire* that separated and rested on each one of them. Then they were all filled with the Holy Spirit and began to speak in different tongues, as the Spirit enabled them. (Acts 2:1-4, emphases mine)

When we allow ourselves to live a life on fire, imbued with his fire, the winds of the Holy Ghost blow and start more Holy Ghost wildfires. When we live life submitted to the process of refining and surrender, attacks will still come, but it will be much harder for the Enemy to quench the fire in us. Putting out a wildfire is much harder than putting out a match. So, surrender it all to Christ. Let him ignite you with a new zeal for his will and ways. Let him do a new thing in you. What he has is always better than what we might be holding onto. Too often the things we grasp tightly hold us back and stifle our growth and walk. Give your whole self to him and catch his fire.

Revival in Your Heart

We tend to think of a revival as a kind of chain reaction that only springs up during a church service or special event. We have made this word synonymous with a conference or a planned series of meetings, but if we look up its definition, we gain insight into what revival actually is.

Revival refers to the "act or instance of reviving, the state of being revived" as well as "a restoration of force, validity, or effect (as to a contract), renewed attention to or interest in something."[33] It can be an awakening in a church or a community or a reawakened interest and increased spiritual interest. And then, of course, it also refers to an evangelistic service or a series of services for the purpose of effecting a religious awakening. So, you see it's so much more than just our meetings.

For too long we have been sleeping in the Spirit, moving slow like sloths. We are sleeping through our walk with God, waiting for a revival to come and wake us up and set us on fire. However, revival begins with us. Revival is not about a meeting; it is about the people in the meeting. In the same way we prepare the building for the event, we need to prepare ourselves for the move.

Think back to what it looks like when you walk into a beautifully organized conference. Banners are hung beautifully, and decorations are perfectly placed to match those banners and the theme. Everything is clean and smells good. The speakers and schedule have been put in order. Lovely and nutritious dinners and luncheons have been prepared and are waiting to be served. The childcare is all lined up, so you can enjoy the services. All you have to do is relax and take it all in.

But before you got there, there was a lot of preparation that demanded hard work and intense planning. You never saw all the people that scrubbed the toilets, cleaned the floors, and hung all those decorations. You are unaware of the person who stood for hours peeling potatoes and preparing meat. You were not part of the months of prayer and fasting

---

33. "Revival Definition & Meaning," Merriam-Webster (Merriam-Webster), accessed June 1, 2022, https://www.merriam-webster.com/dictionary/revival.

that preceded this day. You did not attend all the organizing meetings, which went into preparing this conference for you!

This is exactly what we need to be doing in our heart: preparing ourselves by aligning ourselves with God so the Holy Spirit can move in us.

> Now Saul was consenting to his death. *At that time a great persecution arose against the church which was at Jerusalem;* and they were all scattered throughout the regions of Judea and Samaria, except the apostles. And devout men carried Stephen to his burial and made great lamentation over him. As for Saul, he made havoc of the church, entering every house, and dragging off men and women, committing them to prison. Therefore, those who were scattered went everywhere preaching the word. *Then Philip went down to the city of Samaria and preached Christ to them.* And the multitudes with one accord heeded the things spoken by Philip, hearing and seeing the miracles which he did. For unclean spirits, crying with a loud voice, came out of many who were possessed; and many who were paralyzed and lame were healed. *And there was great joy in that city.* (Acts 8:1-8 NKJV, emphases mine)

During this time of great persecution, there was still great joy in the city. Regardless of the backdrop of death and imprisonments, the light of revival still penetrated the darkness that attempted to stop the early church. We know that his light shines in the darkness, and the darkness cannot overcome it. We can apply this idea to the events of our time too and secure ourselves in the hope and promise that despite the uncertainties that flourish around us, we have this constant truth. No matter what dark powers are trying to operate in our world, nothing will stop God from moving. Nothing will stop his church from growing. And nothing can stop a revival once it starts.

Like we said before, many things go into preparation behind the scenes. Each part may seem small, but they all work together to bring about the bigger picture. What if I told you that something happened in Samaria years before that made a way for Philip to preach Christ to them?

Therefore, when the Lord knew that the Pharisees had heard that Jesus made and baptized more disciples than John (though Jesus Himself did not baptize, but His disciples,) He left Judea and departed again to Galilee. *But He needed to go through Samaria.*

So He came to a city of Samaria which is called Sychar, near the plot of ground that Jacob gave to his son Joseph. Now Jacob's well was there. Jesus therefore, being wearied from His journey, sat thus by the well. It was about the sixth hour. A woman of Samaria came to draw water. Jesus said to her, "Give Me a drink." For His disciples had gone away into the city to buy food.

Then the woman of Samaria said to Him, "How is it that You, being a Jew, ask a drink from me, a Samaritan woman?" *For Jews have no dealings with Samaritans.* Jesus answered and said to her, "If you knew the gift of God, and who it is who says to you, 'Give Me a drink,' you would have asked Him, and He would have given you living water." The woman said to Him, "Sir, You have nothing to draw with, and the well is deep. Where then do You get that living water? Are You greater than our father Jacob, who gave us the well, and drank from it himself, as well as his sons and his livestock?" Jesus answered and said to her, "Whoever drinks of this water will thirst again, but whoever drinks of the water that I shall give him will never thirst. But the water that I shall give him will become in him a fountain of water springing up into everlasting life." The woman said to

Him, "Sir, give me this water, that I may not thirst, nor come here to draw." (John 4:1-15 NKJV, emphases mine)

The receptive hearts Philip found in Samaria all started with a conversation between Jesus and the woman at the well. That was the preparation for this move of God.

> And at this point His disciples came, and they marveled that He talked with a woman; yet no one said, "What do You seek?" or, "Why are You talking with her?" The woman then left her waterpot, went her way into the city, and said to the men, "Come, see a Man who told me all things that I ever did. Could this be the Christ?" Then they went out of the city and came to Him. (John 4:27-30 NKJV, emphases mine)

The roots of this revival were founded on uncommon ground. First, Jesus being a Jew was talking to a Samaritan, and a Samaritan *woman* for that matter. In Bible times, women were to be seen and not heard by cultural standards. Jesus cared for none of those things, and he saw what the world did not. He still does. Purpose. Destiny. Meaning. Those are his focal points in each of our lives.

> And many of the Samaritans of that city believed in Him because of the word of the woman who testified, "He told me all that I ever did." So when the Samaritans had come to Him, they urged Him to stay with them; and He stayed there two days. And many more believed because of His own word. Then they said to the woman, "Now we believe, not because of what you said, for we ourselves have heard Him and we know that this is indeed the Christ, the Savior of the world." (John 4:39-42 NKJV, emphases mine)

Jesus reaped souls for the kingdom that day, but he also planted seeds for something greater to happen in the future. He told the Samaritan woman this: "But the hour is coming, and now is, when the true worshipers will worship the Father in spirit and truth; for the Father is seeking such to worship Him. God is Spirit, and those who worship Him must worship in spirit and truth" (John 4:23-24 NKJV).

In that moment Jesus looked past the shadow of the cross to the glorious day when the church would be born, and the true worshipers of the Father would worship him in Spirit and in truth as guided by the indwelling Holy Spirit. That is exactly what happened years later.

> Now when the apostles who were at Jerusalem *heard that Samaria had received the word of God,* they *sent Peter and John to them,* who, when they had come down, prayed for them that they might receive the Holy Spirit. For as yet He had fallen upon none of them. They had only been baptized in the name of the Lord Jesus. *Then they laid hands on them, and they received the Holy Spirit. (*Acts 8:14-17 NKJV, emphases mine)

Let's return to the woman at the well again. It is extremely prophetic that while this woman was testifying to her townspeople about what Jesus had told her, Jesus was teaching his disciples about the principles of sowing and reaping and its effect on the harvest.

> You know the saying, 'One plants and another harvests.' And it's true. I sent you to harvest where you didn't plant; *others had already done the work, and now you will get to gather the harvest."* (John 4:37-38 NLT, emphasis mine)

Wow! I wonder if Peter and John knew in that moment when Jesus was teaching them that they would return to Samaria to gather the harvest that Jesus had just planted. Who would have thought that a conversation with an immoral woman would lead to all of this? This woman was as bad as she could get, especially for back then. By worldly standards, she had pretty much checked all the boxes for the "Do Not Associate with These People" list. But *Jesus still chose her*, and that simple conversation was the single spark that lit the wildfire of revival in Samaria. Everyone is important. You do not know the effect long-term of your words, your encouragement, or the wisdom you share with others.

The Lord's plans are highly strategic. What the world views as a waste of space, like this divorced woman sitting at a well, God views as vital to his plan. For us to pour into others, we must be able to look past what our natural eyes see and worldly ideas we hold, so we can see people from God's perspective. We need to wake up as a church. We have been stuck in the same old patterns for far too long. If we want to go places, we have never gone before, we must do things that we have never done before. It's time for a new thing!

Everyone is important.

Furthermore, knowing the time, now is the moment to awake from sleep. For now our salvation is nearer than when we believed. The night is far spent, the day is at hand. Therefore let us take off the works of darkness and put on the armor of light. (Romans 13:11-12 MEV)

The *Benson Commentary* explains that the phrase "knowing the time" in this passage means the following:

The season, that it is the morning of the day of the gospel, a season of increasing light and grace, but hasting away: that now it is high time to awake out of sleep—Out of that sleep into which you had fallen during the darkness of heathenism, or *before your illumination by divine truth and grace;* that state of insensibility of, and unconcern about, things spiritual and eternal in general, and your own salvation in particular; *to awake to a sense of the infinite importance of the truths and duties revealed to you* in the gospel, and of the near approach of death and judgment, which will put a period to your state of trial, and fix you in a state of final and eternal retribution. It is therefore high time that you should labor, to the utmost of your power, *to improve every opportunity of receiving and doing good,* and of prosecuting the great business of life) which is to secure the favor of God, *a conformity to his image, and your own everlasting happiness.*

Let us therefore *cast off the works,* only suitable to, or excusable in, a state of darkness—That is, *let us abandon all manner of wickedness* which is wont to be practiced in the night, or in a state of ignorance, error, and folly; and let us put on the armor of light—For, *being soldiers, it is our duty to arm and prepare for fight,* inasmuch as we are encompassed about with so many enemies. In other words, let us be clothed with all Christian graces, which, like burnished and beautiful armor, *will be at once an ornament and a defense to us,* and which will reflect the bright beams that are so gloriously rising upon us." (emphases mine)[34]

It is high time we woke up, suited up, and prepared our hearts for not only revival, but for the fight at hand. Do we plan to sit around, doing nothing, just waiting for a fresh revival to fall on us when our Lord returns? We should be like the virgins who were wise and have our lamps trimmed, ready, and full of oil. Instead of being like the foolish virgins who were out buying their oil when the Bridegroom came. Remember, like the wind, oil represents the Holy Spirit.

34. Joseph Benson, "Benson's Commentary," Romans 13:11 commentaries: Do this, knowing the time, that it is already the hour for you to awaken from sleep; for now salvation is nearer to us than when we believed., accessed June 1, 2022, https://biblehub.com/commentaries/romans/13-11.htm.

But *while they went to buy some*, the bridegroom came, and those who were ready went in with him to the wedding banquet. And the door was shut. (Matthew 25:10 MEV, emphasis mine)

We cannot live off old oil, and we cannot use someone else's either. We must be getting ready ourselves. We should be preparing for not only a great awakening, but also for Christ's return. No one can do this for us. We can be exposed to even the greatest move of the Holy Spirit, yet still be that one person that does not sense the flow and the fire. People may bring the fire, but we must be ready to receive and move in it. We have to start a freshness within. Put out the garbage, cleanse our temples, and renew our lives and walk.

Psalm 51:10 says: "Create in me a clean heart, O God, and renew a right spirit within me" (ESV). A right spirit or steadfast spirit in Hebrew is *kun* which means "to be firm."[35] It's related to the roots include determined, established, get yourself ready, make preparation, reliable. According to Strong's Exhaustive Concordance certainty, confirm, direct, faithfulness, fashion, firm, be fitted.

This is not just a beautiful song we sing. We truly need a clean heart from God and a steadfast spirit. We should wake each day, seeking after Christ and striving to be more like him. We should be head over heels in love with him and his Spirit. There is no one else like him in all the earth. He is the one who should be your first, your last—your everything. We must wake up spiritually. It is time to start hungering and thirsting for him.

I stretch forth my hands unto You; my soul thirsts after You as a thirsty land. Selah. (Psalm 143:6 MEV)

As the deer pants after the water brooks, so my soul pants after You, O God. (Psalm 42:1 MEV)

---

35. James Strong, "3559. Kun," Strong's Hebrew: 3559. כּוּן (kun) -- to be firm, accessed June 1, 2022, https://biblehub.com/hebrew/3559.htm.

> On the last and greatest day of the feast, Jesus stood and cried out, "If anyone is thirsty, let him come to Me and drink. He who believes in Me, as the Scripture has said, out of his heart shall flow rivers of living water." (John 7:37-38 MEV)

We need to let Jesus give us a spiritual heart transplant and let his living water flow through us. It is like a faucet; you can have a trickle or a full stream. You can even shut it off. The Holy Spirit wants to flow like a river in us. Are you willing? You have to be willing, because he will not force you. He is a gentleman. I do not know about you, but I want revival in my heart, my home, my church, my car—everywhere. I want to be someone that brings the Spirit with me, who has revival fire already burning in my heart.

It is time to start catching fire. In the *Hunger Games,* Katniss is called "the girl on fire."[36] They were making something beautiful out of a lump of dirty coal. Jesus wants to take your ashes and make something beautiful too. Do you want to be the man or woman on fire in the Spirit? It's a great goal to be that person who hears this when they walk into a room: "Hey, there's _____! They are on fire for the Lord!"

> John answered them all, "I indeed baptize you with water. But One mightier than I is coming, the strings of whose shoes I am not worthy to untie. He will baptize you with the Holy Spirit and with fire. (Luke 3:16 MEV)

> For our God is a consuming fire. (Hebrews 12:29 MEV)

The Greek word for fire is *pyr,* and it means "God's Spirit, like a holy fire, enlightens and purifies so that believers can share more and more in his likeness. Indeed, the fire of God brings the uninterrupted privilege of being transformed which happens by experiencing faith through Christ. Our lives can become true offerings to him as we obey this imparted

---

36. Suzanne Collins, *The Hunger Games* (New York: Scholastic Press, 2008).

faith from God by his power. This is illustrated by God's fire burning continuously at the entrance of the tabernacle where the priests made sweet offerings (Leviticus 6:12-13, 1 Peter 2:5,9)."[37]

Do you want to see revival? Do you want to see the Spirit flow? Do you want to see deliverance, healings, miracles, and the return of prodigals? Do you want to see victory in your battle? Then wake up and *catch his fire.* Let it spark in your heart. Let it grow, give in to it. Let it purify and refine you; let it consume what needs to be gone. Then go out and spread it!

We are conduits of fire to each other! A conduit is a means of transmitting and distributing. Catch the fire! Be the fire! Spread the fire!

Let revival blaze in your heart!

---

37. James Strong, "4442. Pur," Strong's Greek: 4442. πῦρ (PUR) -- fire, accessed June 1, 2022, https://biblehub.com/greek/4442.htm.

15

What Are You Building?

P roverbs 14:1 says that "the wise woman builds her house, but the foolish pulls it down with her hands" (NKJV). What a sobering image. We can build our house (spiritually or naturally), and we can actually tear it down. It is hard work to build something. It takes time, sacrifice, and labor. Imagine going through all that work only to tear it down later. We love to blame the Enemy when our homes come tumbling down; and not only do we blame him, but we often point the finger at our brothers and sisters in Christ too. Just like Adam and Eve. Their experience when God confronted them was the first round of the blame game.

> And He said, "Who told you that you were naked? Have you eaten from the tree of which I commanded you that you should not eat?" Then the man said, "*The woman whom You gave to be with me,* she gave me of the tree, and I ate." And the Lord God said to the woman, "What is this you have done?" The woman said, "*The serpent deceived me,* and I ate." (Genesis 3:11-13 NKJV, emphases mine)

Adam even had the audacity to blame God when he said, "The woman *whom You gave* to be with me" was the reason for his failure to obey God. In other words, if You hadn't given her to me, I wouldn't have eaten the fruit.

It's easy to look at this situation and think, "How foolish it was for Adam to blame his wife or blame God, or for Eve to blame the serpent!" However, I have fallen into this trap too, thinking: "If God would have done this, then I would not have done what I did. I only did what I did because of what they said/did. I was only reacting to what they did." At the end of the day, it comes down to accepting responsibility for our choices. No one can make us do anything that we truly don't want to do.

> Let no one say when he is tempted, "I am tempted by God"; for God cannot be tempted by evil, nor does He Himself tempt anyone. But each one is tempted when he is drawn away *by his own desires* and enticed. Then, when desire has conceived, it gives birth to sin; and sin, when it is full-grown, brings forth death. (James 1:13-15 NKJV, emphasis mine)

It's our own desires that lead us into sin. We need to check our hearts and evaluate our desires. Does our desire add to what God is building in us, or does it tear it down? What in our flesh is causing us to make the choice to destroy what we want in the spirit? The first step is accepting our own faults. We don't like to admit when we are wrong, but in the long run, we are only hurting ourselves by our own dishonesty. Adam and Eve's foolish blame-shifting is the same as ours.

> Delight yourself also in the Lord, and He shall give you the desires of your heart. (Psalm 37:4 NKJV, emphasis mine)

This is a promise that most of us know. Unfortunately, it gets misused. We cannot apply this promise to our lives if our desires are not godly. God will not give us desires that are contradictory to his character. It's also important to note that the word "delight" carries with it the idea of being pliable and moldable to the will of God.[38] The more we let God mold us, the more our desires will line up with his desires.

> Do not be deceived, my beloved brethren. Every good gift and every perfect gift is from above, and comes down from the Father of lights, with whom there is no variation or shadow of turning. (James 1:16-17 NKJV)

God only gives good and perfect gifts. Our desires can be the very thing that destroy us if they are not good ones and built on a solid foundation. We build this foundation by saturating our mind with the Word of God.

> For the word of God is living and powerful, and sharper than any two-edged sword, piercing even to the division of soul and spirit, and of joints and marrow, *and is a discerner of the thoughts and intents of the heart.* (Hebrews 4:12 NKJV, emphasis mine)

Digging into the Word and allowing the sword of the Spirit to pierce you will help you discern the intents of your heart.

> The way of the just is uprightness; O Most Upright, You weigh the path of the just. Yes, in the way of Your judgments, O Lord, we have waited for You; *the desire of our soul is for Your name* and for the remembrance of You. *With my soul I have desired You in the night,* yes, by my spirit within me I will seek You early; for when Your judgments are in the earth, the inhabitants of the world will learn righteousness. (Isaiah 26:7-9 NKJV, emphases mine)

---

38. James Strong, "2656. Chephets," Strong's Hebrew: 2656. חֵפֶץ (Chephets) -- delight, pleasure (biblehub), accessed June 15, 2022, https://biblehub.com/hebrew/2656.htm.

Having a desire for God is what delighting in the Lord looks like. When our desire is Christ, it leaves little room for the Enemy to come in and tempt us; and we won't be deceived into making choices that will tear down what we are trying to build. Not everything is the Enemy's fault or other people's fault, and most certainly not God's fault. Many of our failings come down to our choices based on our desires.

> The wise woman builds her house, but the foolish pulls it down *with her hands.* (Proverbs 14:1 NKJV, emphasis mine)

Note the wording: her hands. Not her husband's hands, not the Devil's hands, and not some rude stranger's hands. Her hands. Her choices. On the other hand, the wise woman builds. The word "wise" here is the Hebrew *chokmoth* which simply means wisdom, but comes from *chokmah*, which refers to "wisdom (in a good sense), skillful, wisdom, wisely, wits."[39] Start by asking yourself these questions:

- What are you building?

- What do you want to build?

- Are you tearing down what you're building?

- Are you building your temple, or are you building a tower of pride like the people who built the tower of Babel?

- Are you building your home, or are you building yourself?

- Are you building a ministry, a marriage, a church?

- Are you building an inheritance to leave to your family?

- Are you building a dwelling place for the anointing?

No one starts building a house, gets nearly completed, and then demolishes it and starts over! Why would we do that? If we are doing

---

39. James Strong, "2451. Chokmah," Strong's Hebrew: 2451. חׇכְמׇה (Chokmah) -- wisdom, accessed June 1, 2022, https://biblehub.com/hebrew/2451.htm.

> Those who built on the wall, and those who carried burdens, loaded themselves so that with one hand they worked at construction, and with the other held a weapon. Every one of the builders had his sword girded at his side as he built. And the one who sounded the trumpet was beside me. (Nehemiah 4:17-18 NKJV, emphasis mine)

As we are building, we need to be on alert and ready to fight. We must be diligent.

> I will take my stand at my watchpost and station myself on the tower, and look out to see what he will say to me, and what I will answer concerning my complaint. (Habakkuk 2:1 ESV)

We are to stand on top of our tower, watching. Some of the meanings for "watch" are "to look out, spy, keep watch, to watch closely."[40] If we are doing that, we are staying alert like a wise woman. I love what it says next: We are "to see what he will say" and what I will answer. Don't be hasty. If we are, we will end up tearing down our house. We will have to wait and see what he says to us, and trust his timing and wisdom, even if we do not understand it, and we rarely do.

Unfortunately, we often tear down more than we think in our lives. Half the time, we don't even realize we are doing it. Sometimes I think we notice it, but don't know how to stop it. For some of us, it's all we know.

> A continual dripping on a very rainy day and a contentious woman are alike; whoever restrains her restrains the wind, and grasps oil with his right hand. (Proverbs 27:15-16 NKJV)

---

40. "Watch Definition & Meaning," Merriam-Webster (Merriam-Webster), accessed June 1, 2022, https://www.merriam-webster.com/dictionary/watch.

The *Tyndale Life Application Daily Devotion* for these verses says this refers to "quarrelsome nagging, a steady stream of unwanted advice is a form of torture."[41] People nag because they think they aren't getting through, but nagging hinders communication more than it helps! My mind was blown. My father had been the ultimate nag. He could have written a book on it. I remember begging him to stop. I'd ask him to just ground me, so I didn't have to listen to him no more. Even though I hated it in him, I learned this negative behavior and practiced it as I grew. I did this to my husband more than once. What a destructive habit! It tears down what you have built.

Nagging hinders communication.

Here's an example: Recently I was reminding my husband of how he promised to quit smoking. He is convinced that e-cigarettes and vaping is not the same as smoking, so he told me that he had. My blood boils when he tells me that, so I started nagging, "You promised you would nineteen years ago! The whole time I was pregnant, and while the twins were in the NICU, you said you would do it, but you haven't!..." By this time, he was sitting down, but I didn't stop. I said, "Do you want the boys to think it's okay? What's wrong with you?" I was unrelenting and would not let it go. Eventually, my husband got very angry. Now we have to go Jericho march around with each other but because both of us are annoyed and barely talking. We weren't in a spiritual posture. I did not use words of love and patience; I was not being wise. I set off a stick of dynamite in the very house I was trying to build. Should that result have surprised me? I'm in a process of growth and I am learning to make better choices.

> Wives, likewise, be submissive to your own husbands, that even if some do not obey the word, they, without a word, may be won by the conduct of their wives, when they observe your chaste conduct accompanied by fear.

41. Life Application, Life App, and the Life App logo are registered trademarks of Tyndale House Ministries. © 2020 Tyndale House Publishers.

> Do not let your adornment be merely outward—arranging the hair, wearing gold, or putting on fine apparel—rather let it be the hidden person of the heart, with the incorruptible beauty of a gentle and quiet spirit, which is very precious in the sight of God. (1 Peter 3:1-4 NKJV)

It says they can be won "without a word"; they can be won by our conduct! The word "fear" in verse two translates to "reverence"; it continues, urging us to have a gentle and quiet spirit. We are talking about our spouses here, but the same can be applied to our children, family, friends, and ministries. We can talk until we are blue in the face and tell others what great Christians we are, but they are watching our conduct. Our conduct speaks volumes. The Bible tells us that we will know people by their fruit. Our fruit exposes us. If we are being counterfeit, it will show. People are watching to see how we are going to act and respond.

Consider the person that sits in church and seems engaged. Throughout the meeting, they are clapping, shouting hallelujah, and have their hands raised to God. However, the minute the service is over, they're speaking ill of another or gossiping about someone else's hardship. What message does that send to the unsaved who are watching? Would they want what is being built? Don't get me wrong, we are all works in progress. We all fall short, but we have to learn to grow. Like G.I Joe "knowing is half the battle.[42]

Our conduct speaks volumes.

Our responses will build, or like a hammer, knock our building down. When we are in the ministry, we need to pay extra attention because if we aren't building the kingdom up, we just might be tearing it down—only now we are doing it publicly and teaching others to do the same thing. We should not preach and minister our hearts out, letting the Spirit flow, only to go to a party and gossip about others. What message does it send if you are leading worship on Sunday, and prancing around

42. G. I. Joe is a licensed trademark and media franchise that is owned and produced by the Hasbro Toy Company.

in a string bikini like you'd see in *Maxim* magazine on Monday? Or what if after someone asks you to pray for them, you put them down to someone else after the fact? These behaviors will not make people want what you have! What if you're the only Bible someone meets? Would knowing you make them want to build with the Lord?

> Let no unwholesome word come out of your mouth, but if there is any good word for edification according to the need of the moment, say that, so that it will give grace to those who hear. (Ephesians 4:29 NASB)

We need to quit tearing each other down with our words and instead build one another up in Christ. We need to learn to guard our mouth! Guard our mind! Guard our heart! We must watch our attitude and our actions: Do they build up or tear down? Your family may not hear what you say, but they will see what you do! What are you showing them?

Ask yourself today whether you are building a tower of pride, or an ark of safety, obedience, and faith like Noah. Are you building a land of rebellion and lies like Saul, or a heart of repentance and worship like David? Are you building the home of a Proverbs 31 woman? I know I want to do that.

What are we building? Christians, or sinners, love, or hatred? Are we building others up or are we tearing them down? Are we building the body of Christ today? Or are we building for the world?

> So then, let us aim for harmony in the church and try to build each other up. (Romans 14:19 NLT)

We must always remember that we are not called to build our own empire; we are called to expand the kingdom of heaven. Church and the gifts God has given us should never turn into a competition. We are many members of one body—each with a purpose and a plan. When we start to "brand" ourselves and our gifts and seek the praise of man, we are creating a foothold for the Enemy to tear down the church from the inside out. We must be careful of our motives and keep ourselves in check. Jealousy, pride, and greed can tempt us into making poor choices. We should never compete with our brothers and sisters in the body of Christ. This tears down the church. Instead, we should be encouraging them to dive deeper into their gifts and deeper into their relationship with Christ. We should celebrate their gifts and build them up. It is never about us, but about Jesus, and his gifts were given for the edification of the whole body.

What are you building? Your empire or his kingdom? One of those is worth building; the other is just sinking sand.

> ## We are not called to build our own empire; we are called to expand the kingdom of heaven.

What we build matters more than we could ever imagine. Through the pages of this book, we have pointed out many of the little foxes that creep in, spoiling our vine and bringing down what has been built from the inside. Most of us never understood how fast these little things can spoil the good. Do we want to leave that kind of example for our families, friends, and acquaintances?

Think of each one of these items as a brick in your house. The negative ones are not strong, but weak. They are riddled with stress fractures, and eventually they will break and crumble. Now imagine that for every small (and large) issue you clean up in your life, you receive a new brick in its place. A beautiful and strong one that supports the structure. When you submit to God's process, your house will be better—bigger and stronger.

After reflecting on everything you have read, are you willing to let the Holy Spirit do a good work in you? Are you ready to start being purified? If you are willing, he is able! It is worth it! Pruning isn't a fun process, but it brings the next season's harvest!

I don't know about you, but as for me and my house, we are going to serve the Lord and build on a firm foundation, living a life consecrated to the Maker of heaven! All else is sinking sand.

The choice is yours, and yours alone. He's waiting, knocking at the door of your heart, but you must open it. You must make the choice: whether good or bad, right, or wrong. It's up to you. Will you join me, and open the door and choose to be refined?

The Little Foxes

By HelenAnn

It's the little foxes that spoil the vine:
Extremely deadly when you give them time
To crawl in the back doors, the windows, the cracks,
So very innocent until they attack.
They look so small, so cute, and so shy,
Until their fangs grow, and they plan how you die.
Ravenous hunger is their nature's call,
And it's uncontrolled; they are beasts, after all.
We think we have power over their natural design,
But it's we who are fools for forgetting our vines.
Tempted by the what ifs, the thrills, and the pleasures,
The little foxes come and steal all of our treasures.
Our choice brought them in, gave them refuge, a box,
But never forget: *A fox is a fox.*

About the Authors

Alicia

Alicia is the mom of miracle twins, for whom she warred and waited, for nineteen years. She is a wife and a lover of God's Word, and a Bible study teacher for ten years and counting. The founder of Armed and Anointed Ministries, she is currently studying to become an ordained minister under Cornerstone Ministries in Bear, Delaware. Her heart is to see Christians walk in their full potential and according to all the promises that God has given them, and to help them wield their weapons properly to defeat the Enemy through the power of the trinity.

HelenAnn

HelenAnn is a housewife and dog-mom from Arizona. She is the producer for Armed and Anointed Ministries and the cofounder for Kingdom Bound Worship, a compilation praise and worship album, dedicated to show-casing original work from the hidden gems of contemporary Christian music. Her heart is for teaching, but her passion is for worship. A pen is often in her hand, writing songs or books, but when she is not writing, she is adjusting to her new life in the Wild West after moving from the Finger Lakes region of upstate New York. She misses the lakes, but loves the mountains, and is very happy with this new chapter God has granted her.

Armed and Anointed Ministries

Armed and Anointed gives Bible study teachings and scriptures to help fight your battles to war for your life family and friends. I have walked through fire, and God walked me through. We will help you learn how to walk with God through the fire

To join the Armed and Anointed group on Facebook, go to https://www. facebook.com/groups/221637872516469/ or use the QR code below.

Or visit us on Instagram:

ARMED_AND_ANOINTED_MINISTRIES

Check out our YouTube channel at https://youtube.com/channel/ UC2q0QY28QJu0FTDP5VfwIBg.

CPSIA information can be obtained
at www.ICGtesting.com
Printed in the USA
BVHW041417300323
661447BV00003B/436

9 798987 267608